APPLIQUÉ!

APPLIQUÉ!!

THE COMPLETE GUIDE TO HAND APPLIQUÉ

APPLIQUÉ!!!

LAURENE SINEMA

THE QUILT DIGEST PRESS

Published in the United States of America by The Quilt Digest Press.
Editorial and production direction by Bill Folk.
Production management by James Nelson.
Editing by Jan Johnson and Janet Reed.
Technical editing by Kandy Petersen.
Cover copy by Sharon Gilbert.
Book and cover design by Kajun Graphics, San Francisco.
Diagrams and illustrations by Sally Shimizu and Kandy Petersen.
Photography by Sharon Risedorph, San Francisco.
Photograph on page 8 by Chance Houston.
Typographical composition by DC Typography, San Francisco.
Printing by Nissha Printing Company Ltd., Kyoto, Japan.
Color separations by the printer.
Second Printing

Library of Congress Cataloging-in-Publication Data

Sinema, Laurene.
    Appliqué! Appliqué!! Appliqué!!! / by Laurene Sinema.
        p.   cm.
    ISBN 0-913327-38-7
    1. Appliqué—Patterns.   2. Patchwork quilts.   I. Title.
TT779.S57   1992
746.9'7—dc20   92-24026
                                                              CIP

The Quilt Digest Press
P.O. Box 1331
Gualala, California 95445

To Michael Kile who had a vision and allowed me to fulfill it.

I give a heart full of thanks to:

The Quilted Apple staff who tended the shop faithfully over many months

The Quilted Apple Club

The Quilted Apple Masters Class

Betsy Viator, Jill Pace, Lynda Brown, Diane Ebner, and Carol Meka who shared editing, computer, and drafting skills

Kay Hunzinger, Joy Jung, Betty Alderman, and Ann Cardon who started it all

Family, friends, and students in Phoenix and beyond who listened, listened, and listened

Ardis and Robert James who generously loaned their antique quilts

Editors Jan Johnson, Janet Reed, and Kandy Petersen who gently urged me forward

Illustrator Sally Shimizu who gave my primitive drawings credence, beauty, and clarity

The Quilt Digest Team: Bill Folk, James Nelson, Sharon Gilbert, and Jeff Bartee, who showed constant care and enthusiasm

The following manufacturers and suppliers: American Classic Fabric, RJR Fabrics, Hoffman Fabrics, P&B Fabrics, Robert Horton Plaids, Pat Andreatta, and Fairfield Processing Co.

My husband, Gerry, who lightened the load with love

CONTENTS

Friendship Album Quilt, *made by staff and students for Laurene Sinema*

INTRODUCTION

YOU MIGHT SAY THAT *APPLIQUÉ! APPLIQUÉ!! APPLIQUÉ!!!* WAS CONCEIVED about fifteen years ago. Of course, I didn't know then that I would be writing this book now. Nor did I imagine that so many people in my home state of Arizona and around the country would be so interested in making the beautiful and traditional art of appliqué their own.

What happened then is Janet Carruth and I met with some friends and decided the state of Arizona should have a quilters' guild. So we called together people from all over the state in the summer of 1977. We sent them home to talk to their friends and fellow quilters, and the next spring in Phoenix we had the first official meeting with about seventy-five quilters. Today there are chapters all over the state and about nine hundred members.

Another project Janet and I have been involved in over the years is the Arizona Quilt Project. Working primarily with eleven other women, and many more volunteers, we've documented over three thousand quilts made before 1940 that "live" in Arizona. The result is an incredible array of styles and colors and a history of our pioneer state. The Project doesn't relate directly to this book, but it sure whetted my appetite to research quilts, particularly appliquéd quilts.

About the same time the Arizona Quilters' Guild formed, Janet and I decided that quilters in Phoenix needed a shop and a place of their own. So we opened The Quilted Apple, which is now, I believe, among the ten largest quilting shops in the country. Every year at The Quilted Apple we run about two hundred classes where two thousand people come to learn to quilt and to appliqué. I take that as evidence that lots of people are interested in quilting and in appliqué, which has become the love of my quilting life.

In the early days of The Quilted Apple, I taught appliqué mainly because somebody had to do it. In the process I learned about all kinds of techniques, and I became particularly interested in traditional Hawaiian appliqué.

We also brought Elly Sienkiewicz, who had just begun work on her Baltimore Album book, *Baltimore Beauties and Beyond,* to The Quilted Apple to teach two workshops. She then *very* graciously consented to send me her material before it was published so I could continue teaching.

I was driven to learn all I could about both the history and the techniques of appliqué so I could pass that information along to my students. There were times when I barely stayed ahead of my students in drafting designs, researching, and learning techniques I could then teach them. In fact, I often didn't have time to finish whole projects. So I would work a piece until I knew the technique, then I'd begin several blocks to use in classes. I'd often finish only a quarter of each block before the class got underway. That's how I became known as the Queen of Quarter Blocks, a nickname that has stuck to this day.

Through researching midnineteenth-century appliqué, I became fascinated with the traditional and fine Baltimore Album specimens. But I became even more fascinated with the primitive, and in some ways more creative, folk-art quilts from that period. All of that and more is reflected in this book.

When I teach, my mission is to immerse people into the techniques, the way it was "really" done. That's why I teach the techniques from the 1840s—tack and chain stitches and colonial knots, particularly. I want everyone to become proficient at the techniques. I think if my students don't go beyond my teaching then I haven't done my job. I've constructed this book to help you go beyond. I've included a whole array of appliqué techniques from the nineteenth century to the present and from a variety of cultural traditions. I've devoted an entire chapter to stitches because appliqué, after all, begins with stitches.

But I'm not interested in simply recreating history. I want to do innovations on tradition. Quilting truly is a folk art, like folk music. People learn one pattern or technique, just as they learn one melody line or set of lyrics in folk music. As folk music is passed along, people often add other lyrics or expand on the melody line. The same thing can happen with quilts.

In this book, I've given you some of my innovations. For instance, the *Hawaiian Sampler Quilt* is a quilt of my design, based on traditional Hawaiian technique and design. I have no desire to take away from the original Hawaiian designers; I want to teach their techniques and designs to my students, who can use today's fabrics and ideas to make something new and beautiful based on the old.

The *Easter Lily Quilt* is another example. I took the design from a block done by Carrie Hall, who sent it as a surprise to Emma Andres on Easter in 1942. I added to it, updating the colors a bit and giving it cornerstones and a scalloped border for a more contemporary look.

The stained glass project in this book is yet another example. Traditional stained glass has lots of flowers and angels in it. I wanted to do something different and more contemporary looking. So I came up with combining two traditions: I set a traditional Della Robia wreath, which is of course not usually done this way, in stained glass. Then I designed the whole thing to be done in bright, contemporary colors. I think you'll like the effect.

I've written complete construction guidelines for each project. And I've included information about finishing projects, for how disappointing it is to complete a block or a quilt top and then not know the best way to finish it.

I've shared some of my story and the background that brought me to write this book. I must introduce you to one more person. This book would never have come to be without Laura Nielson, my father's mother for whom I am named, for it was she who first instilled in me a love of quilting and other crafts.

She thrust a crochet hook into my hand before I could read. (To this day I take a full-fisted approach to handling a crochet hook, which is probably why you're reading a book about appliqué rather than crochet written by me.) She patiently taught me the embroidery stitches I now use in appliqué. I worked my way up from samplers and dish towels to table linens. She taught me to piece quilts, and she taught me the technique of appliqué much used then, buttonhole over raw edges, which looks pretty primitive today. And if she hadn't worked so patiently with me so many—we won't say how many—years ago in Paul, Idaho, I wouldn't be doing the work I'm doing today.

Appliqué techniques exist worldwide. I have no doubt that the origin of appliqué was utilitarian and lowly. After all, what is appliqué but a patch, putting one piece of fabric over another, perhaps to cover a hole, to make do, to make something last longer? That is women's way. But it's also women's way to create beauty and peace. Working an appliqué piece soothes the soul. With each stitch you take—and you take thousands, maybe millions—you leave your cares behind as you concentrate on the work in front of you. And you create beauty as you go.

I truly believe our inner souls long to be creative. We each put something of our creative selves into every piece we work. And appliqué, with its curves and swoops and points and circles, many of them following nature and everyday life, stirs my inner creative spirit in a way no geometric piecing ever could.

This book, and my life, have been enriched by the cooperation and friendship of hundreds of people. I've mentioned some of them by name in the acknowledgments and in the introductions to specific quilts. Appliqué has also enhanced my life in so many ways. The quilt you see on page 8 reflects one of those ways. It's a *Friendship Album Quilt* created for me by students and friends from The Quilted Apple.

Several of the blocks are original designs. The *scherenschnitte* (paper cut) apple, center block, top row was designed by Penny Dimick from Phoenix. For this quilt, it was appliquéd by Carol Meka and Heidi Eberenz, also from Phoenix. Betty Alderman, from Mansfield, Ohio, designed another original paper cut, the first block on the left in the middle row. She also designed and made the stylized cornucopia, second row, second block.

Next to that block, the center block in the second row, is another original, an apple tree under an apple arbor, designed and appliquéd by Kay Eneim from Tempe, Arizona. The pictorial block, center in the bottom row, depicts in paint the first and second homes of The Quilted Apple—a red barn on a busy Phoenix street and a charming house on an equally busy street. The trees framing the picture are a fabric border for the block created by Marilyn Phillips of Phoenix.

The two blocks on either side of it are made from large prints, one a green floral, the other a red paisley. Both add a contemporary flavor to the quilt. The second block from the left on the bottom is a pineapple by Peg MacDonald of Scottsdale, Arizona. And the red star was made by Sharon Robinson of Peoria, Arizona.

Just above the pictorial block is a cornucopia filled with fruit made from contemporary fabrics that give it an almost folk-art appearance. Seventy-year-old Irma Adams, from Phoenix, appliquéd this whimsical block.

Several women who worked on the quilt have moved from the Phoenix area. I just want to make sure I mention them. Joy Jung and Betty Alderman went to Ohio; Lauri McKay to California; Susan Lawler to Massachusetts; and Audrey Waite to Sedona, Arizona.

The winding feather, quilted as the sashing between each block, was designed by Carol Meka. Ruth Umble, from Glendale, Arizona, put the final stitches on the quilt as she spent some 850 hours exquisitely hand quilting the feathers and the quarter-inch crosshatching. This beautiful quilt chronicles the lives of its makers and records the very nature of human existence, in that we cannot say and do not know with certainty what tomorrow holds for each of us.

I love this quilt so much that I took one of the blocks, the basket of flowers, to create a project especially for this book. You'll find it in chapter 11, Nineteenth-Century Traditional Appliqué.

My fondest hopes for this book are that you will use it to learn and re-fine appliqué techniques, that you will be enchanted by the patterns and work some of them, *and* that you will take what you learn from this book and begin to work with innovations of your own.

The quilts in this book include a range from easy to extremely challeng-ing, for everyone from beginner to master. There are traditional patterns and techniques, and there are some original creations.

Remember that the techniques are always the same. It is experience that carries you from beginning to master level. Carefully following the instruc-tions in this book will help you to produce beautiful and satisfying results, even if you haven't done much appliqué.

Those of you new to appliqué will want to work with designs containing gradual curves, larger circles, wider points, and larger pieces. At the inter-mediate level, choose designs with more complex shapes, smaller circles, and narrower points.

The advanced quilts in this book have more intricate designs—for exam-ple, narrow bias stems, smaller shapes, deep curves. And for the master, there are challenging miniature and large elaborate designs, with tiny circles, very sharp points, and layered shapes.

Appliqué! Appliqué!! Appliqué!!! is organized into chapters by style. There are a couple of ways to use the book. First, if you want to master all of the techniques, begin in chapter 3 with the *Heart Sampler Quilt.* Each block of this quilt is done in a different style of appliqué.

Second, you may choose to do a project from one (and then hopefully more) of the other chapters. Choose a full-sized quilt, wall quilt, or cradle coverlet. There are twenty to choose from in styles ranging from traditional to contemporary, from techniques used around the world.

Before you begin a project, it's crucial that you read through the basics in the next two chapters. As you work the projects in the book, these chapters will help you, and you can refer back to them as you learn and become skilled at each new technique.

Throughout the text, I have shared hints I've come across in my fifteen years of doing and teaching appliqué to make your appliqué easy, satisfying, beautiful, and, most of all, enjoyable. So, before you begin, remember:

1. Read Essentials and Stitches, and become acquainted with the overall information necessary to any appliqué project. Collect all the equipment and supplies as outlined so you will be totally prepared as you begin your project.

2. Choose the appliqué style you'll work on first. Study each chapter until you find the style or the quilt you wish to create. If you're a beginner, you may want to practice the necessary technique by beginning with the *Heart Sampler* block in chapter 3 associated with your chosen quilt project. If you wish to become proficient at many different techniques—and end up with a beautiful wall quilt—you may want to complete the entire *Heart Sampler Quilt.*

3. When you've completed the appliqué, finish the quilt. You can refer to chapter 13, Finishing, for instructions.

Good luck! Have fun! My wish for you is that you love every stitch as much as I do.

Chapter 1

~

THE ESSENTIALS

VOCABULARY

GLOSSARIES ARE OFTEN AT THE BACK OF THE BOOK WHERE THEY GET LOST. I'VE put this one up front because by reading through it first you'll begin to become familiar with the terms I use in the following chapters.

APPLIQUÉ. From the French word *appliquer,* which means "to put on or lay on; a cut-out decoration fastened to a large piece of material." That's the dictionary definition; it doesn't begin to describe the variety and beauty of the design, shapes, pictures you can create with this technique.

BACKING. Bottom fabric layer of the quilt.

BASTE. Loose running stitches used to hold the three layers of the quilt or two layers of fabric together.

BATTING. Filler between the top and back of the quilt.

BIAS. A line diagonal to the grain of fabric, or a narrow strip of fabric cut on the bias.

BINDING. Narrow strip of fabric added to the edge of a quilt as the finish—it can be cut on the straight grain of the fabric or on the bias.

BORDER. The final strip or number of strips added to the edge of the quilt top.

BUTCHER PAPER. White paper, 36″ wide, usually purchased at an art supply store.

DIAGONAL SETTING. See ON POINT.

DRESSMAKER'S CARBON. Paper with a special finish on one side used to transfer pattern lines onto fabric.

EMBROIDERY. Surface stitchery embellishment.

FREEZER PAPER. Paper with a poly-coated finish on one side; used as a template.

GRAIN. The direction that threads run in woven fabric: threads that run parallel to the selvage are lengthwise grain; threads that run perpendicular to the selvage are crosswise grain.

GROUND OR BASE. Fabric that motifs are sewn onto.

MEDALLION. A style of quilt with a central block surrounded by several borders.

MITRE. Strips of fabric sewn together at a 45-degree angle to form a corner.

MOTIF. Shapes to be applied to ground fabric.

NEEDLETURN. Turning the seam allowance under using a needle or toothpick.

ON POINT. The diagonal position of a quilt block in the final assembly of the full top.

OVERLAY. The top layer of fabric used in shadow and reverse appliqué.

PATTERN. The overall plan or picture for a block or quilt.

QUILT. (n): A bed cover consisting of a top, filler, and a back held together with quilting stitches. (v): To sew together with a running stitch, usually in a pattern, the three layers of a quilt.

QUILT TOP. The top layer of a quilt or coverlet. A quilt top can be appliquéd, pieced, or a single piece of cloth.

REVERSE APPLIQUÉ. Appliqué technique of cutting away layered fabric to expose lower colors.

SASHING OR LATTICE. Strips of fabric joining blocks into a quilt top.

SET. The way blocks are arranged to be sewn into a quilt.

SHADOW APPLIQUÉ. A style of appliqué using a sheer fabric over solid colored motifs and ground fabric. By stitching around the edges of the motifs through all three layers, the appliqué motifs are softened into shadows under the sheer overlay fabric.

TEMPLASTIC. A sturdy transparent plastic used to make templates.

TEMPLATE. The pattern piece used as a guide for cutting patchwork and appliqué pieces and for marking quilting.

UNDERLAY. The bottom layer of fabric used in reverse appliqué.

WHOLE CLOTH QUILT. A quilt with top and backing made of single large pieces of fabric, with batting sandwiched in between.

Equipment and Supplies

You'll need most of the equipment and supplies on this list for each of the projects in this book. I've put the list in the front of the book because it is best to know about and gather your supplies before you begin a project.

1. BALL-POINT PEN, empty
2. BIAS BARS
3. BUTCHER PAPER
4. CIRCLE TEMPLATE (PLASTIC)
5. C-THRU PLASTIC RULER
6. DRESSMAKER'S CARBON
7. FABRIC GLUE STICK
8. FREEZER PAPER, (POLY-COATED)
9. LIGHT BOX
10. MARKING PEN
11. NEEDLE THREADER
12. NEEDLES, size 7 embroidery, size 11 sharps, size 8 quilting or betweens
13. PENCILS, white chalk, yellow chalk, no. 2½ lead
14. PINS, ¾″ sequin, glass head
15. SCISSORS, small sharp pointed, 8″ fabric, paper cutting
16. TAG BOARD OR INDEX CARDS
17. TEMPLASTIC
18. THIMBLE
19. THREAD
20. TOOTHPICKS, round
21. TRACING PAPER

FABRICS

CHOOSING FABRICS

MEASUREMENTS: Most fabrics in America come on 45″-wide bolts. I'll use this as the standard in the yardage section to each quilt. If you need to know the metric equivalent for any measurement, multiply the inches by 2.54.

GROUND OR BASE: Choose a 100 percent cotton, good quality off-white muslin or my preference, American Classic™—an off-white polished cotton that gives all projects a lovely patina that adds to the beauty of the quilts.

If you just love white or feel the quilt you are planning must have a white ground, please remember that white tends to make the design seem smaller. Therefore, you may wish to enlarge your design so the ground fabric is less overwhelming. Or you may choose from the large number of white-on-muslin or white-on-white designs available.

APPLIQUÉ MOTIFS: Choose 100 percent cotton prints or solids. You must choose fabrics that will hold the necessary crease as the motifs are appliquéd onto the ground fabric.

BORDER: Choose 100 percent cotton solids or prints in the same fabric as the backing or one of the appliqué motifs or in a complementary color or pattern.

BATTING: The antique quilts included in this book all have 100 percent cotton batting. Most of these quilts have been quilted heavily, and thin batting makes that easier. The antique Hawaiian quilt, with slightly thicker batting, is the exception.

The new quilts have fairly thin batting because I like a thin batt. You may prefer a slightly thicker batt to get a puffier look. If so, please choose one for your quilt.

We are fortunate to live in a time when many types and thicknesses of batts are available. Your local quilt shop will give you information and help concerning the different manufacturers and the features of each brand. The batt should extend at least two inches beyond all four sides of the quilt top. You'll trim away the excess after the quilting is completed and one side of the binding has been stitched onto the quilt.

BACKING: Choose 100 percent cotton solids or prints that combine well in color and design with your quilt top and that please you. The lengthwise grain line of the backing fabric should run the length of the quilt to keep the quilt straight through many washings. All the yardage measurements in this book are the length of the quilt times the number of widths it will take to make the backing. When two widths are needed, the second width is cut in half lengthwise and sewn to either side of the center width. One center seam is more vulnerable especially if the quilt is large. When three widths are used, they are all cut the same width and sewn together with two seams.

BINDING: The binding you choose for a quilt, wall quilt, or table topper is determined by the thickness of your batting and by whether the quilt has a straight or curved edge. You must use bias binding on quilts with curved edges. You may use either straight-cut or bias binding on all other quilt edges.

The antique quilts in this book all have straight-cut bindings and very thin batts. If you desire to have your quilts look like the antique quilts, use straight-cut binding as suggested in the cutting instructions.

PREPARING FABRICS

PRESHRINKING: Treat the fabric as you will the finished project. Use cold water, a small amount of soap, and the gentle cycle of your washing machine. Dry the fabric in the dryer if you will dry the finished product in the dryer. Press. NOTE: Be sure your fabric is smooth and wrinkle free. Test the fabrics you think may not be colorfast. Either discard them or wash them several times to prevent any discoloration of your quilt.

If I'm working on a project that will not ever be touched by water I do not preshrink the fabrics. I enjoy working with the fabrics "fresh from the bolt." I also realize the value of the quilt that is in pristine condition—unwashed and little used. So for my heirloom quilts, I never wash the fabrics.

WORKING WITH FABRICS

GRAIN LINES: If you understand and use the grain lines and bias of fabric, working with your fabric motif will be easier. And your final project will look more pleasing.

Here's a simple way to determine the grains. When you pull on the *lengthwise grain,* the fabric will not stretch. When you pull on the *crosswise grain,* the fabric will have a bit of stretch. However, when you pull on the *diagonal of the grain* or *bias,* the fabric will have a great deal of stretch. *(See diagram 1.)*

With this information, you can use any scrap of fabric without the benefit of the selvage as a guide. Just pull the fabric, and the bias and the grain lines become obvious.

In appliqué, placing the templates on the fabric using the grain lines properly means less clipping will be necessary on curves, because the bias stretches.

GROUND OR BASE: Remember, the ground is the background fabric to which the appliqué fabric motifs are applied. An appliquéd block tends to be smaller than its original cut size (the stitches seem to eat up the fabric). So, when you cut your ground piece, it's a good idea to add one inch to each side of the pattern size. The measurements given in the Cutting instructions in each quilt include this additional allowance. After cutting the ground to proper size, fold the fabric into quarters and then diagonally into eighths. The eight creases will guide you in placing the fabric motifs. *(See diagram 2.)*

I seldom draw on the ground fabric; I just do not like to see pencil lines after the appliqué is completed. You may wonder how I keep the appliqué motifs in their proper places. In most cases the ground fabric is a light color and easy to see through. So I simply place a full-size pattern under the ground fabric, align the creases, and use it as a guide for the motifs. I pin a few motifs in place and stitch them. Then I place the ground over the guide again to pin and stitch a few more. When the ground is a dark fabric, I use a daylight window or a light box with the pattern under the ground fabric as before.

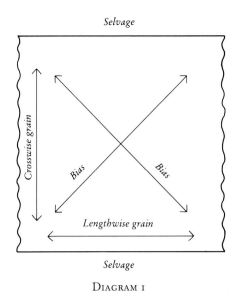

DIAGRAM 1

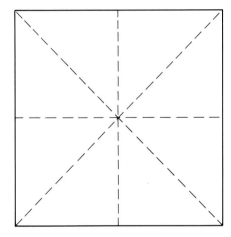

DIAGRAM 2

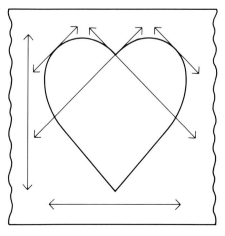

DIAGRAM 3

APPLIQUÉ MOTIFS: Motifs are the shapes of fabric to be applied to the ground or base. You must study each motif template before you place it on the fabric. Always lay the template on the fabric using the grain lines to your advantage. *(See diagram 3.)*

To prevent extra creasing and possibly stitching your block to itself, hold your work in this manner as you appliqué: Roll the outside edge nearest your work area into a small cylinder that will rest in the hollow of your hand between your thumb and forefinger. Be sure to roll the wrong side *up* onto the top of the work.

PATTERN PREPARATION

FULL-SIZE BUTCHER PAPER PATTERNS

You must have a full-size pattern to appliqué a block, a border, or a whole cloth quilt. The pattern will be placed under the ground fabric and used constantly to guide the proper placement of the fabric motifs. In some of the quilts you may wish to use the pattern directly from the book. However, I find that to be awkward and not as mobile as a separate pattern. I use butcher paper to make my patterns.

Trace the entire design on the paper using a black fine-point marking pen. Make larger designs in sections on separate pages, and assemble them into a full-size pattern. Fold the pattern into quarters and then diagonally into eighths, just as you folded your ground fabric. Matching the fold lines will help you accurately place the motifs.

BORDER PATTERNS: The patterns for appliquéd borders include a corner and a portion of a side. Make a corner of butcher paper, following the instructions in the individual quilt, and trace the design onto it. Matching the center of the prepared border fabric to the center of the repeating section of the border, trace the pattern onto your fabric from this point. Work toward the corners, moving the pattern as necessary. Depending on the size of your quilt, you may have to adjust the design on your fabric to make the transition into the corner smooth.

ABOUT TEMPLATES

FREEZER PAPER: My favorite template material is freezer paper. I first learned of this method from Baltimore Album expert Elly Sienkiewicz and I use it almost exclusively. You will find this paper in the supermarket in the same area you find wax paper and aluminum foil. Be sure to purchase poly-coated freezer paper, not waxed. (The paper template is ironed onto the right side of your fabric. You will be extremely unhappy if you use waxed freezer paper as a wax residue remains.) A drawn line is necessary to guide you as the stitches are taken.

1. Place the shiny side of the paper on the pattern. Trace all motif shapes with a no. 2½ lead pencil.

2. With paper-cutting scissors, cut out all shapes on the drawn line. REMEMBER: The shape you cut is the shape you appliqué, so take care and cut accurately.

3. Place the shiny side of each template on the right side of the fabric. REMEMBER: Use the grain lines to your advantage. Leave ½″ between the templates.

4. Press with hot iron, no more than 10–15 seconds in any one place. The paper will stick to your fabric.

5. Draw around the templates with a white pencil or lead pencil. REMEMBER: You must be able to see the lines as you stitch.

6. Remove the freezer paper. The templates can be used two or three times, so you may wish to save them in an envelope.

7. Cut out the shapes adding a ³⁄₁₆″ seam allowance.

8. Place the motif on the ground fabric, pin or baste, turn under the seam allowance, and stitch.

TAG BOARD, INDEX CARD, OR TEMPLASTIC: Many of the quilts in this book have repeat designs. Each block in the quilt is the same, so the templates used must be of firmer stuff. In this situation, I like to use templastic because the edges remain stable after drawing around them numerous times. When you use tag board or index cards you will have to redraw and cut new templates as the edges begin to shred. REMEMBER: Redraw from the original pattern. Do not trace around a template to prepare a new one, because the size of the new template will end up larger than the original.

1. Place the templastic on the pattern. Copy all motif shapes with pencil or pen—either will do, just be sure you can see the line.

2. With paper-cutting scissors cut out all shapes on the drawn line. REMEMBER: The shape you cut is the shape you appliqué, so take care and cut accurately.

3. Place the template on the right side of the fabric. REMEMBER: Use the grain lines to your advantage and leave ½″ between the templates.

4. Draw around the templates with white pencil or lead pencil. REMEMBER: You must be able to see the lines as you stitch.

5. Cut out the motifs adding a ³⁄₁₆″ seam allowance.

6. Place the motif on the ground fabric, turn under the seam allowance, and stitch.

FREEZER PAPER—ON TOP: I have several students (excellent appliquérs) who prefer not to draw lines, but to leave the freezer paper template on top of the motif fabric. They fold the seam allowance under, letting the edge of the freezer paper be the guide. A minor miracle happens when you fold under the seam allowance. The freezer paper will not allow the fabric to fold completely under and a wee edge is left for you to stitch into.

1. Place the shiny side of the paper on the pattern. Copy all motif shapes with a no. 2½ lead pencil.

2. With paper-cutting scissors cut out all shapes on the drawn line. REMEMBER: The shape you cut is the shape you appliqué so take care and cut accurately.

3. Place the shiny side of each template on the right side of your fabric. REMEMBER: Use the grain lines to your advantage. Leave ½″ between the templates.

4. Press with a hot iron, no more than 10–15 seconds in any one place. The paper will stick to the fabric.

5. Cut out the shapes adding a ³⁄₁₆″ seam allowance.

6. Place the motif on the ground fabric, turn under the seam allowance, and stitch.

One disadvantage to this method is that as you hold the work to appliqué, the rolling and unrolling of the excess ground material causes the template to pull away from the motif. Sometimes you can iron the template down again, sometimes you cannot. Plus, *there is no line to follow on the fabric.* As a matter of personal preference I do not use this method. However, since so many people find it useful and I want this book to be comprehensive, I include it here. You will want to experiment with these methods until you find the one that works best for you.

DIAGRAM 4

PAPER BASTING: Another method I don't often use, but you may be interested in, is the paper-basting method. This method is especially useful in appliquéing circles.

1. Prepare regular paper patterns by tracing motif shapes and cutting on the drawn lines. REMEMBER: The shape you cut is the shape you appliqué, so take care and cut accurately.

2. Use the patterns to cut out your fabric motifs. NOTE: Add a ³⁄₁₆″ seam allowance, and remember to use the grain lines to your advantage.

3. Place a pattern on the wrong side of a fabric motif, fold the seam allowance over the paper pattern, and baste through both fabric and paper pattern, easing the fullness as necessary.

4. Appliqué the paper-basted motif onto the ground fabric; stop the appliqué 1″ before completing the motif.

5. Remove the basting stitches and pull the paper pattern out.

6. Complete stitching the motif.

ENLARGING AND REDUCING PATTERNS

Most copy machines will enlarge or reduce by percentages to the size desired. Enlargement percentages are specified in the individual patterns at the back of the book. Or you may use the graph method. I have used this often and find it works well if I don't have a copy machine available.

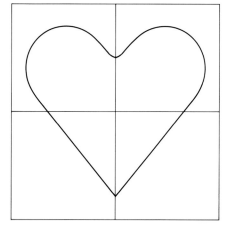

DIAGRAM 6

Determine the size you wish to enlarge or reduce your pattern to, and measure a paper to that size. Mark off units on your original pattern. *(See diagram 4.)* Mark the same number of units on your paper. Now transfer the design to your paper by drawing in each square the corresponding lines from the original into smaller or larger squares, depending on whether you're reducing or enlarging. *(See diagrams 5 and 6.)*

BIAS PREPARATION

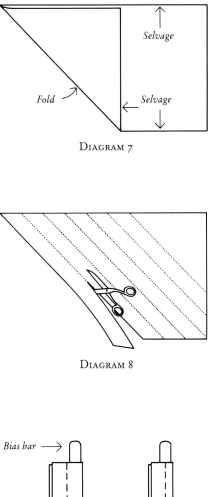

When my four daughters were tiny and I sewed all their clothes, I was unaware of the small amount of fabric needed to make a large amount of bias. So I would always purchase an extra yard of fabric just for the bias. I had yards of leftover fabric before I figured out I didn't need much to make bias strips.

Many times you will need only a short length of bias and will want to make it out of a small piece of fabric. When you do, here is a quick formula to determine the length of bias strip you can get from any size square of fabric: 1½ times the length of one side of the square. This isn't exact, but it's close enough and quick, plus very easy! Of course, depending on the width of the bias strip, you can get many more than one length from the piece of fabric.

Another fact that escaped me for years was that a rectangle of fabric can be used as well as a square. So don't take a perfectly good rectangle and cut off one end to form a square. It is a waste of the fabric, especially if you need more bias.

SHORT LENGTHS FOR VINES, STEMS, AND SUCH

1. Place a square or rectangle of fabric on a flat surface. Square up the left side and fold the bottom left corner to the top edge to form a right angle. Crease fabric. *(See diagram 7.)*

2. With ruler and scissors, measure and cut bias strips. Use the width measurement given in the cutting instructions for your specific quilt. *(See diagram 8.)*

3. You will have short separate strips for stems and vines.

TUBES FOR VINES, STEMS, CELTIC, OR STAINED GLASS

1. Prepare bias strips as described above.

2. Fold bias strip in half lengthwise *right* side *out* and place a bias bar inside, next to the fold. NOTE: Bias bars by Pat Andreatta come in the narrow widths used in this book and can be purchased in most quilt shops.

3. Place the edge of the bias bar against the zipper foot on your sewing machine and stitch with small stiches. Slide the bias bar down the bias strip if necessary as you continue stitching. *(See diagram 9.)*

4. Turn the seam to the back of the bias bar and press it to one side. *(See diagram 10.)*

5. With the bias bar inside the tube, trim the seam so it will not peek out under the tube as you appliqué. Remove bias bar.

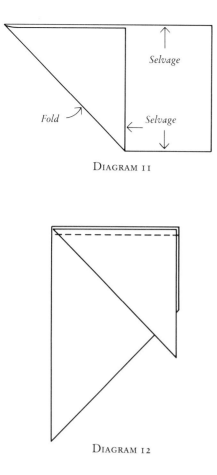

DIAGRAM 11

CONTINUOUS STRIPS FOR
BINDINGS AND LONG VINES

A 45″ square of fabric will yield about 20 yds. of 1½″ bias.

1. Place a square or rectangle of fabric on a flat surface. Square up both ends and fold the bottom left corner to the top edge to form a right angle. Crease fabric. Cut fabric on crease. *(See diagram 11.)*

2. Place right sides together, matching the squared-up ends, and stitch on sewing machine, using tiny stitches and a ¼″ seam allowance. *(See diagram 12.)*

3. Press seam open. Measure and mark with a pencil, on the wrong side of the fabric, the desired width of bias strip across the length of the seamed fabric. *(See diagram 13.)*

4. With right sides together and raw edges even, match marked lines—*offset* marks so the top edge of one end aligns with the first marked line of the other end. Pin, matching all marks, and sew to form a tube. *(See diagram 14.)*

5. Cut fabric along marked lines in one continuous spiral. *(See diagram 15.)*

DIAGRAM 12

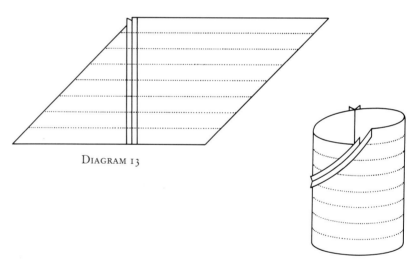

DIAGRAM 13

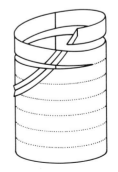

DIAGRAM 14

DIAGRAM 15

REVERSE APPLIQUÉ

I just want to take a moment to introduce you to reverse appliqué, which we'll use in the mola, Pa ndau, Hawaiian, and nineteenth-century quilts. In this style of quilting, you layer one or several pieces of fabric on the ground fabric and cut away portions of the upper layers to expose the lower and ground fabrics.

BASIC REVERSE APPLIQUÉ INSTRUCTIONS

1. If the design is simple, prepare templates using one of the methods detailed in About Templates page 20 (the best method is freezer paper). Place the template on the right side of the overlay and trace around it with a pencil. Be sure to mark all areas that will be reversed out.

If the design is intricate, like the mola or Pa ndau, the most accurate method for transferring the design to the overlay is to trace it. With a light overlay fabric, you should be able to see the pattern through the fabric. If your overlay is dark, use a light box or a daylight window to help you see the pattern lines. Again, be sure to mark all areas that will be reversed out.

2. With small sharp pointed scissors, make a small snip in the section to be reverse appliquéd before you place the overlay on the ground fabric. NOTE: You *need* a tiny snip to put the scissors into at the time you cut away to appliqué. (Without the snip you might cut all the way through several layers!) *(See diagram 16.)*

3. With right sides up, center the overlay on ground fabric. If there are several layers, sandwich them into the proper places now. Small pieces can be tucked into openings as you appliqué.

4. Depending upon the amount of reverse appliqué, pin or baste through all layers.

5. Carefully cut away the overlay material to expose the lower layers, retaining a ³⁄₁₆″ seam allowance to be turned under. *(See diagram 17.)*

6. Turn under seam allowance on drawn line using a round wooden toothpick.

7. Starting at an inside curve, with seam allowance turned under, appliqué around entire opening. NOTE: Clip curves and corners as needed. *(See diagram 18.)*

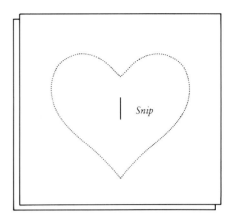

DIAGRAM 16

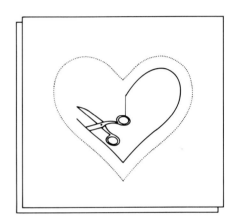

DIAGRAM 17

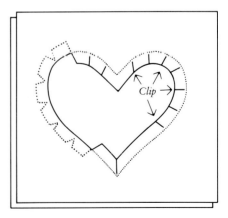

DIAGRAM 18

Chapter 2

∼

THE STITCHES

ONE OF THE BEAUTIES OF AN APPLIQUÉD QUILT IS THE STITCH USED TO APPLY the motif fabric to the ground fabric. In some quilts it is a decorative stitch—a stitch that is visible and is *meant* to be visible, a stitch that adds beauty and dimension to the design. The running stitch and buttonhole stitch are two decorative stitches you will learn. A few embroidery stitches are also found on appliqué quilts and are used to emphasize the appliqué motif. I have included the outline stitch, chain stitch, and colonial knot—the most common decorative embellishment stitches.

To hand appliqué and not have the stitches "show" is the goal of almost every appliquér. The tack stitch and the ladder stitch make that goal attainable. All these stitches, with step-by-step instructions, are presented here for you to learn and refer to whenever you may need them.

For all decorative and embellishment stitches thread a size 7 embroidery needle with one 2-ply strand of embroidery floss. (NOTE: Floss comes as a 6-ply strand: Separate out and use only 2-ply.) Thread should not be longer than 18″. Tie a knot in one end of the thread.

For tack and ladder stitches thread a size 11 sharp needle with a single strand of size 60 machine embroidery thread. Your thread should be the color of the appliqué motif and about 18″ long. Tie a knot in one end of the thread.

If you are right-handed, work the stitches from right to left. If you are left-handed, work the stitches from left to right. The only exception is the outline stitch, which everyone will work left to right.

RUNNING STITCH

Did you learn the running stitch as a child as I did? My grandmother taught me when I was probably only four or five years old. A little person does this stitch by the jab method—needle up, needle down—much the same as cross stitch. The problem with this method is that the stitches usually look uneven, especially when a beginner is stitching.

The true secret to success with this stitch is to take several stitches at a time, weaving the needle in and out of the fabric before pulling the thread through, with the needle always ending on top of the project. As you proceed, you tend to gauge the size of the stitch with greater ease and achieve an even stitch.

This stitch is meant to be seen, so determine its length by the size of the motif to be appliquéd. When the motif is large the stitch is large (no larger than ¼″). When the motif is small the stitch is small. Sew ¹⁄₁₆″ to ⅛″ from the folded edge of the motif.

This stitch is fast and easy, running in and out of the motif at regular intervals. With the seam allowance of the motif folded under, start the stitch just inside the edge at A with the needle under the ground fabric. Come up into the motif at A, go down at B, up at C, down at D, and so on. *(See diagram 1.)* All of the stitches on top of the motif and under the ground should be equal in length.

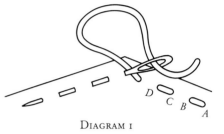

DIAGRAM 1

BUTTONHOLE OR BLANKET STITCH

Most of us recognize the buttonhole stitch. I remember seeing it on quilts, dish towels, clothing, and old-fashioned dresser scarves. It is a versatile stitch in that it can be used with or without turning the seam allowance under as you appliqué. The stitch actually lies along the edge of the motif and hides the edge of the fabric. However, if you intend to wash the article, the edges of the fabric soon fray and tiny threads begin to work through the blanket stitch. Very discouraging to the maker I am sure. So, if you're going to wash your finished piece, do turn under a seam allowance as you stitch.

The stitch has two common names: buttonhole and blanket stitch. If the stitches are very close together, it is called a buttonhole. (That's logical; just look at a buttonhole on your clothing.) When the stitches are taken farther apart, it's called the blanket stitch. For the purpose of reducing confusion, we're going to call this the buttonhole stitch, no matter what its size.

Before you begin the stitch you must determine the size of the stitch you will be taking. Follow the same simple, logical rule we used with the running stitch: When the motif is large the stitch is large. When the motif is small the stitch is small. Make the distance between the stitches the same size as the depth of the stitch. The stitches should be as even as you can make them. Strive for perfection. You can do it!

With the seam allowance of the motif folded under, start the stitch just outside the edge at A.

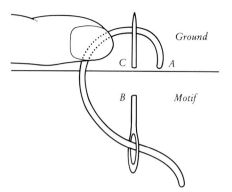

DIAGRAM 2

1. Come up from under the ground fabric at A, so the knot will be on the wrong side of your block. Circle the thread to the left, and hold it down with your left thumb. Insert the needle at B and come up at C. With thread under the point of the needle, pull through. (See diagram 2.)

2. Adjust the thread as a loop is formed. Tension should be snug and even. If you pull too tight the fabric will begin to bunch up between the stitches. If the stitch is too loose, the thread will gap and can easily be snagged on something and pulled out.

3. Continue down at D, up at E, and so on. (See diagram 3.)

Here are some tricks to help you turn corners. (See diagrams 4 and 5.)

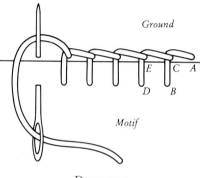

DIAGRAM 3

Round

Watch carefully so you can plan the stitches as you near a curve. They should all be evenly spaced.

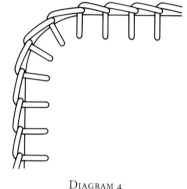

DIAGRAM 4

Square

Watch carefully with square corners also. Place one stitch at A, one at B, and one at C, using the same center hole for all three stitches.

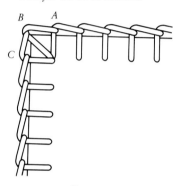

DIAGRAM 5

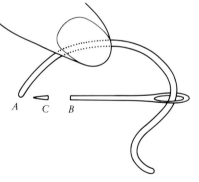

DIAGRAM 6

OUTLINE STITCH

I learned to embroider on a set of dish towels. The little girls on the towels were helping with the chores: one washing clothes, another hanging them on a line. My grandmother sat with me and patiently taught me the stitch I now know as the stem stitch. As an adult, I continued to use this stitch until someone showed and taught me the outline stitch. I was an immediate convert. The outline stitch serves the same purpose as the stem stitch, but it is a more beautiful stitch that looks like a crisp line drawn in ink when it is done properly.

Keeping your stitches tiny will make it easier to turn corners and make curves smooth and true. Draw your embroidery lines on the appliqué motif. You will stitch on the drawn line.

1. Come up from the ground fabric at A, so the knot will be on the wrong side of your work. Holding the thread above the needle with your left thumb, push the needle down at B and up at C. Pull the thread through. (See diagram 6.) The distance from A to B, C to D, and so on is always equal. C should fall halfway between A and B; B should fall halfway between C and D; and so on.

2. Go down at D, and up at B (in the same hole). Make sure to hold the thread above the needle with your left thumb. Pull the thread through, and pull it taut after each stitch. Continue in the same manner. (See diagram 7.)

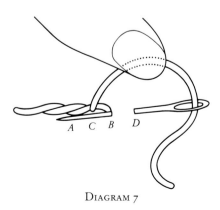

DIAGRAM 7

NOTE: I drag the point of the needle along the wrong side of the completed stitches until it pops into the previous hole. That's an easy way to make the stitch perfect!

CHAIN STITCH

Emma Andres, one of Arizona's master quilters, taught me this stitch on a summer afternoon. We sat together in my den and Emma, with one of her funny little hats perched on her head, told me of the importance of tiny, even stitches. "Take your time, make every stitch the same length," she said. She used the chain stitch to outline and as a filler in close parallel rows in several of her prize-winning quilts.

First draw the embroidery lines on the appliqué motif, then stitch on the drawn line.

1. Come up from under the ground fabric at A, so the knot will be on the wrong side of your block. Circle the thread to the left, and hold it down with your left thumb. Insert the needle at A (in the same hole) and come up at B. With the thread looped under the point of the needle, pull the needle through. *(See diagram 8.)*

2. Adjust the thread as a loop is formed. Tension should be snug. If the stitch is too tight, the threads will pull together and the chain will disappear. If the stitch is too loose the threads will gap and make an uneven chain.

3. Continue down at B, up at C, and so on. *(See diagram 9.)*

4. To end, stitch down over the last chain to anchor it.

COLONIAL KNOT

Centers of flowers and eyes of birds and butterflies traditionally get their texture from the French knot. The French knot is a relatively easy stitch, but you seldom get consistently sized knots. So I prefer the colonial knot, the stitch used in candlewicking in the eighteenth and early nineteenth centuries on all-white counterpane quilts (the thread was the loosely twisted yarn used in candlemaking). This knot is prettier and more uniform. Try it and you will agree. Anita Shackleford, Ohio embroidery embellishment expert, has graciously shared with me her colonial knot instructions. I have adapted them to share with you.

Draw dots on the appliqué design to designate the proper placement of the knot. You will stitch directly on the dots.

1. Come up from under the ground fabric at a dot on the appliqué. The thread knot will be on the wrong side of your work.

2. Place your left thumb on the thread about 1″ away from where the thread comes up. With your right hand, point the needle toward the beginning point, crossing over the thread to the left. Pull the needle back under the thread to the right for the first wrap. *(See diagrams 10 and 11.)*

3. With your left hand, lift the thread over and around the point of the needle to create a figure-8 wrap. *(See diagram 12.)*

4. Insert the needle close to the right of the beginning point, and push the needle straight down. With your left hand, pull on the thread to tighten the knot around the needle. *(See diagram 13.)*

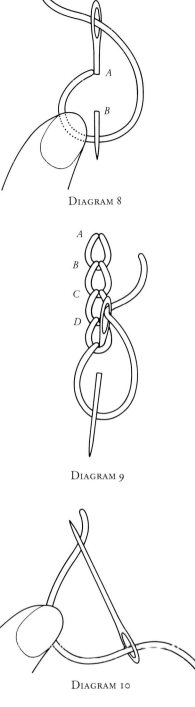

DIAGRAM 8

DIAGRAM 9

DIAGRAM 10

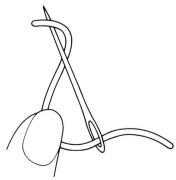

DIAGRAM 11

5. Carefully push the needle through the knot and the fabric to the back and secure. NOTE: When the thread has been adjusted around the needle the knots will always be a consistent size with a tiny dimple in the center. *(See diagram 14.)*

Why don't you try a few colonial knots on a practice piece? The difficulty arises as you hold the wrapped thread. If you do not hold it firmly, the knots will not be uniform. Some will be tiny and tight, others will be large and loose. The ideal is a medium size and a snug tension.

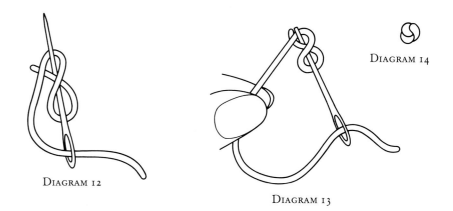

DIAGRAM 14

DIAGRAM 12

DIAGRAM 13

TACK STITCH

The tack stitch is my favorite stitch for hand appliqué. It's the one used in all the finest nineteenth-century appliqué. Almost invisible when sewn correctly, this stitch secures even the most intricate appliqué easily and permanently. I perfected this stitch in a Baltimore Album appliqué workshop taught by Elly Sienkiewicz. I can still hear her saying "Just repeat this little phrase: Up in the green, down in the white." *You* must do the same as you are stitching. Bring your thread up in the motif. Go back down in the ground. And you will have perfect appliqué!

1. Come up from under the ground fabric in the motif at A. (The knot will be on the wrong side of your block.) When the thread comes up at A, I pull it away from me—straight toward the edge of the ground fabric. Working along the top folded edge of the motif, go down at B (straight across from A). *(See diagram 15.)*

2. After the needle is inserted into the ground fabric at B, I turn the needle so it will come up at C in one stitch.

These are very tiny straight stitches taken in the edge of the motif fabric. The advancing stitches are tiny diagonal stitches underneath the ground fabric. The length and distance between the stitches should be no more than ¹⁄₁₆″. REMEMBER: The stitch is practically invisible. For the purpose of explanation, the diagram stitches are exaggerated.

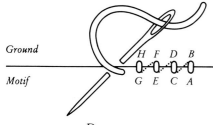

Ground

Motif

H F D B
G E C A

DIAGRAM 15

CORNERS

On the corners, curves, and the tips of points, the stitches will be very close together to prevent the motif fabric from jutting out and fraying.

INSIDE CORNERS:

1. Cut the seam allowance diagonally, all the way into the drawn corner point, with half the seam allowance on the right and half on the left. *(See diagram 16.)*

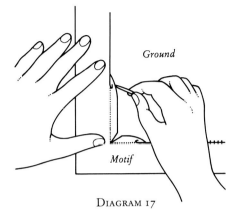

DIAGRAM 17

2. Turn under the seam allowance. Begin stitching toward a corner and sew to within 1″ of it. Now is the time to get out your round wooden toothpick. Place your work flat on the table, and begin turning under the seam allowance on the next side of the corner about 1″ away from the point; work toward your stitching. *(See diagram 17.)* NOTE: The wood fiber of the toothpick catches the fabric, and a minor miracle happens. As you turn the corner, where only threads are left, somehow the toothpick catches those threads and turns them under to create a perfectly square corner.

3. Press this turned-under corner with your left hand. Hold it while you tack stitch to the corner.

4. Take one longer stitch diagonally in the corner and then a second tiny stitch, pulling it up tightly. The corner will be as square as the drawn line. *(See diagram 18.)*

5. Turn the work and continue the appliqué.

OUTSIDE CORNERS OR POINTS:

1. Appliqué up to the drawn corner point, and take two stitches next to each other. You will see the stitches. *(See diagram 19.)*

2. With the round wooden toothpick, turn under the left seam allowance. (The two stitches will hold the corner point taut while you turn under the seam allowance.) *(See diagram 20.)* When it is totally turned under, give a little tug on the thread and the corner will become perfectly square.

3. Turn the work and continue to appliqué.

SHARP POINTS

1. Appliqué up to the drawn corner point, and take two stitches next to each other. You will see one of the stitches. If your seam allowance at the point is more than 3⁄16″, trim away the excess from the top. *(See diagram 21.)*

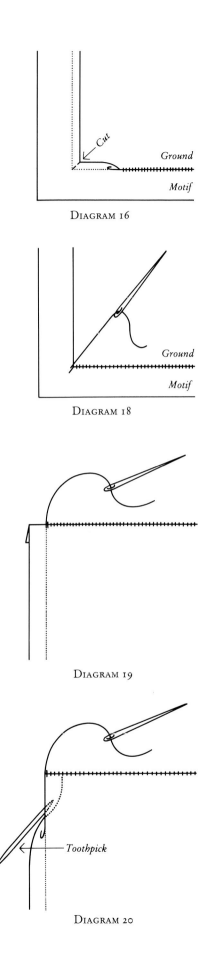

DIAGRAM 16

DIAGRAM 18

DIAGRAM 19

Toothpick

DIAGRAM 20

DIAGRAM 21

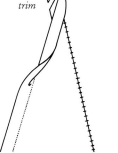

DIAGRAM 22

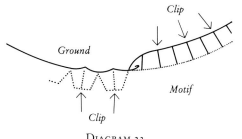

DIAGRAM 23

2. If the point is very sharp, flip the fabric forward and trim away some of the seam allowance on the side of the point that is already stitched. *(See diagram 22.)* Using the round wooden toothpick, turn under the remaining seam allowance, pushing and smoothing until it is all inside the point.

3. Tug on the thread, turn the work, and continue to appliqué.

CURVES

INSIDE CURVES: If you study the diagram of an inside curve you'll see that you *must* clip the edge to allow the seam allowance to spread when it is turned under.

1. Always clip to the drawn line.

2. Always have an uneven number of clips: 3, 5, 7, and so on.

3. After clipping, place the work flat on the table, holding it down with your left hand. Use the round wooden toothpick to roll under the seam allowance, working left to right, toward your stitching. If you do not get a nice smooth curve (a point sprouts or the edge looks square) you must take an extra clip or two. *(See diagram 23.)*

4. Continue to appliqué around the curve. Use your left hand to smooth and finger press the curve.

CURVES:

1. It is not necessary to clip outside curves. The grain of the fabric allows the seam allowance to be easily turned under and appliquéd.

2. Insert the point of the round wooden toothpick between stitches and smooth out any bulk in the seam.

CIRCLES

Antique appliqué quilts from the nineteenth century abound with grapes, cherries, and centers of flowers from very tiny to rather large in size. All of them are circles! And most of them seem to be perfect circles! How can we achieve the beautiful cluster of grapes, stem of cherries, and centers of flowers? Practice, practice, practice!

In examining many antique quilts I have found that not *all* the grapes and cherries on *all* the quilts were perfect. However, when a great number of grapes or cherries are appliquéd on the same quilt and *most* of them are close to perfect, all of them appear perfect. You will do the same thing. Most of your circles will be perfect and *all* of them will appear perfect! Here are two methods to help you achieve perfect circles.

You can also achieve nice round circles using the paper basting method. See page 22 for details.

1. Place a plastic circle template on the right side of your fabric and draw inside the chosen size circle.

2. Add ³⁄₁₆″ or less seam allowance. Cut out. NOTE: If you can "eye-ball" the seam allowance, you do not need to draw the cutting line. Just cut.

3. Pin the circle fabric motif on the ground fabric and appliqué in place using the tack stitch. Do *not* pull your first stitch up tight. Leave it loose so you can ease in any fullness as you take the last stitch. NOTE: Use your round

wooden toothpick to turn under the seam allowance only an inch at a time as you appliqué.

4. Your stitches must be very, very tiny. Watch your drawn line for a perfect circle. NOTE: Place the point of your round wooden toothpick or the eye of the needle through the edge of the stitched circle and use it to distribute the fullness of fabric under the circle.

STUFFED CIRCLES: Use this method for fairly small circles. The additional seam allowance will serve as stuffing for them.

1. Place the plastic circle template on an index card. Draw your circle and cut out on the drawn line.

2. On the wrong side of your fabric, draw the same size circle.

3. Measure the diameter of the circle and add half that number as a seam allowance. Cut out a fabric circle of this size.

4. On the wrong side of the fabric, baste around the circle, half the width of the seam allowance, using fairly large stitches.

5. Place the index card circle template flat on the wrong side of the fabric circle. Pull basting thread to gather the fabric around the template. *(See diagram 24.)*

6. Place the fabric circle with gathers down on an ironing board. Spray with sizing and iron until dry. NOTE: The fabric circle will have a nice crisp edge because the template will serve as a guide.

7. Remove basting thread and template. Pin the fabric motif on the ground fabric and appliqué in place.

DIAGRAM 24

LADDER STITCH

In my high school home-ec class I was taught the ladder stitch to match plaids at the seams of dresses. I thought *everyone* was taught this stitch in every home-ec class in this country. I had a big surprise when I started teaching appliqué using this stitch and very few of my students could do this stitch—or even knew about it.

Use the ladder stitch as an alternative to the tack stitch in appliquéing motifs to ground fabric. The ladder stitch will hold the motif fabric tightly to the ground fabric. Take one stitch in the ground fabric and the next stitch running down the fold of the motif fabric, pulling the fabrics close together.

1. Come up from the ground at A, just outside the top folded edge of the motif.

2. Go directly across into the motif at B. Now, run the needle through the channel of the fold and exit at C. Enter the ground fabric at D, directly across from C. Come up in the ground fabric at E and continue. You may take longer stitches as you travel in the ground fabric and then through the motif channel. *(See diagram 25.)* NOTE: The stitches A-B, C-D, E-F must be taken exactly opposite one another to be invisible. If you happen to stitch on the diagonal, the stitch will be seen. The motif fabric is held close to the ground fabric as the stitches are pulled taut. For corners and curves see instructions in Tack Stitch pages 31–32.

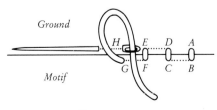

DIAGRAM 25

Heart Sampler Quilt, *appliquéd by Laurene Sinema and quilted by Una Jarvis*

Chapter 3

~

HEART SAMPLER QUILT

ALL THE TECHNIQUES YOU NEED FOR FINE APPLIQUÉ CAN BE LEARNED BY working on a heart shape. An inside point, an outside point, curves, and straight sides—all are found on the heart shape. This sampler quilt was designed to teach you a new technique with each block. The blocks are small and are appliquéd in a short time. The borders take a little longer but are not difficult.

Perhaps you are just beginning to appliqué. If so, start with the running stitch and complete each heart block. By the time you are appliquéing the borders you will be experienced at appliqué and ready for any of the projects in the book.

If you are already experienced you may want to jump right into another project and do the *Heart Sampler Quilt* later.

You will learn the decorative appliqué techniques mola, Celtic, Broderie Perse, shadow, Hawaiian, Pa ndau, and stained glass. Decorative embroidery stitches—running, buttonhole, outline, chain, colonial knot—are included in the blocks along with appliqué stitches—tack and ladder. I had a grand time appliquéing the *Heart Sampler Quilt.* I love green and red! Each block was finished in a short time and looked just as I had planned. The border was especially fun because I enjoy working with bias vines, and the circles were not too difficult. These techniques are included in the instructions. Do try this quilt and have fun!

HEART SAMPLER QUILT

APPLIQUÉ STYLE	Mola, Celtic, Broderie Perse, shadow, Hawaiian, Pa ndau, stained glass
STITCHING TECHNIQUES	Running, buttonhole, tack, ladder, outline, chain, colonial knot
SETTING	Straight set with sashing
FABRIC SUGGESTIONS	
Ground (blocks, borders, binding, and backing)	Off-white solid
Sashing	Off-white solid
Shadow, stained glass, mola, and Pa ndau motifs	Solids
Buttonhole, running, Hawaiian, Celtic, and Broderie Perse motifs	Prints
FINISHED SIZE	38″ × 38″
BLOCKS SET	3 × 3
8″ × 8″ BLOCKS	9

YARDAGE

GROUND (blocks, borders, binding, and backing)	2¾
MOTIFS	
Vine, bias tube	½
All other	¼ each of several fabrics
Voile overlay (1)	10″ square
SASHING	⅓
BATTING	42″ × 42″

CUTTING

GROUND	
Blocks 10″ × 10″	9
MOTIFS	As each pattern dictates
SASHING WIDTH	1½″
BIAS TUBE (1″)	1¼ yds.
BORDER MOTIFS	
Heart leaves	20 of various greens
Cherries	80 of various reds
Vine, bias tube (¾″)	6 yds.
BORDER WIDTH	5½″
BINDING WIDTH	1½″
BACKING	42″ × 42″

1. Prepare one block pattern for each of the 9 heart blocks (patterns are in the back of the book). See Pattern Preparation page 20.

2. Prepare templates for the heart blocks. See About Templates page 20.

3. Prepare fabric shapes using one of the methods detailed in Essentials. NOTE: Add ³⁄₁₆″ seam allowance when cutting.

4. Complete blocks per individual instructions in each section of this chapter. Trim each block to 8½″ × 8½″, centering motif.

5. Set blocks together with sashing. See Straight Set with Sashing in Finishing page 129.

6. Prepare bias tube for vine in border. See Bias Preparation in Essentials page 23.

7. Prepare the border pattern by cutting two 5″ × 30″ strips of butcher paper. Tape them together to form a corner. Copy the design onto paper.

8. Cut borders; see Borders, Mitred page 133. Place the fabric right side up on the pattern. Use a pencil to mark a broken line down the center of the vine for placement of the bias tube. Move the pattern as necessary to mark the entire border. Refer to the photo for placement. See Border Patterns page 20.

9. Starting 9″ from the corner, pin leaves and cherries in place following the pattern and photo. Pin the bias tube following drawn line.

10. Starting on an outer curve, appliqué the vine in place.

11. You may appliqué the entire vine, then leaves and cherries, or you may appliqué as you go—a little vine, a leaf, cherries. You choose! NOTE: Stop appliqué 9″ from the end of the border strip.

12. Continue in this manner, following steps 9–11 until all 4 border strips are completed.

13. Press the borders following instructions in Pressing page 128.

14. Add border strips to quilt top and mitre corners. See Borders page 133 for complete instructions.

15. When the corners are mitred, complete the border appliqué and embroider stems using the chain stitch.

To finish the quilt, see Finishing, chapter 13, for information on pressing your completed quilt top, preparing the batting, preparing the backing, assembling the three layers, quilting, and binding.

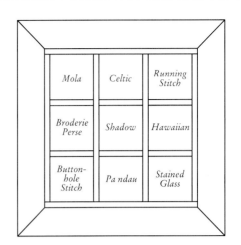

PLACEMENT DIAGRAM

Mola Heart Block

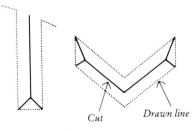

DIAGRAM I

1. Follow step 1 in the *Heart Sampler Quilt* instructions. NOTE: This block will be reverse appliquéd. See page 25 for instructions.

2. Trace entire design on the overlay fabric using a light box or daylight window. NOTE: Mark the areas to be snipped for reverse appliqué according to the pattern.

3. With sharp pointed scissors, make a snip in the center of each of the areas that will be cut away to reveal lower colors. One half of the seam allowance will be turned under and appliquéd on each side of the cut. NOTE: Pattern has lines (—) indicating initial snips.

4. With right sides up, center the marked and snipped dark overlay fabric on top of the off-white ground fabric. Now sandwich the bright colored fabrics between the overlay and ground fabrics in the proper places. Baste the entire design through all the layers. NOTE: Do *not* baste where the snips have been taken.

5. Begin reverse appliqué in the center of the heart at no. 1 to expose the gold fabric beneath. Stitch down both sides of the cut line. NOTE: Cut down the center rectangles and v's stopping ⅛″ from the end and cutting into the corners with diagonal cuts. *(See diagram 1.)* Using a round wooden toothpick, turn under seam allowance. Finger press, and appliqué using the tack stitch. NOTE: I place the work down on a flat surface often and smooth it to prevent puckering.

6. Repeat step 5 beginning next at no. 2 and then at no. 3 to expose all of the gold fabric.

7. Reverse appliqué the inside heart starting at no. 4 to expose the red in the same manner.

8. Reverse appliqué the next heart starting at no. 5 to expose the white ground fabric.

9. Reverse appliqué the outside dark green heart to the ground fabric. Discard the remaining dark overlay.

10. Remove all basting threads. Press the completed block. See Pressing page 128.

11. Embellish with colonial knots as shown in the photograph.

CELTIC HEART BLOCK

1. Follow step 1 in the *Heart Sampler Quilt* instructions.

2. Center the block of ground fabric right side up on the pattern, and draw a broken line down center of the fabric design with a sharp lead pencil. NOTE: You will be able to see the design through the off-white ground fabric.

3. Prepare bias tube: Cut 1″ bias to finish ¼″ wide. See page 23. You will need about 1¼ yds.

4. Starting at no. 1 on the pattern, place the bias tube on the drawn broken line to measure the correct length. Leave a tail of 1″ at the beginning and the end. Pin only an inch or two at a time as you stitch the bias tube in place. NOTE: Pin *over* the bias tube, not *through* it.

5. Appliqué the outside edge using either the ladder stitch or the tack stitch, following the curves of the design.

6. Where the bias tube goes over itself leave an opening to pull the tube through. You will appliqué this opening later.

7. When you reach the bottom of the heart (no. 2 on the pattern) cut off the tail, leaving just enough to lie flat under the bias tube. Appliqué in place through all layers.

8. Continue in this manner until you reach no. 3 on the pattern. Now appliqué beginning again at no. 3 on the inner curve, continuing around the design and ending at no. 1.

9. At no. 4 and no. 5 on the pattern take a tiny tuck on the inner edge to form the point.

10. Go back and appliqué the openings that were left for the tube to cross under itself.

11. Press the completed block. See Pressing page 128.

RUNNING STITCH HEART BLOCK

1. Follow steps 1, 2, and 3 in the *Heart Sampler Quilt* instructions.

2. Center the block of ground fabric right side up on the pattern and pin heart 1 in place.

3. Using a round wooden toothpick, turn under the seam allowance on an outer curve of the heart shape. With the seam allowance folded under, appliqué using the running stitch. NOTE: Choose threads of contrasting color and keep the stitches even. You want them to be seen as a decorative addition to the block.

4. Continue the appliqué with hearts 2, 3, and 4 on top of heart 1, following the pattern. Where the motifs overlap, the lower motif edge should be left flat.

5. Press the completed block. See Pressing page 128.

BRODERIE PERSE HEART BLOCK

1. Follow steps 1, 2, and 3 in the *Heart Sampler Quilt* instructions.

2. Place the heart on the ground fabric. Using a round wooden toothpick, turn under seam allowance on the outer edge of the heart motif. Finger press.

3. Start appliqué at no. 1 on the pattern using the tack stitch.

4. Continue in this manner around the entire heart. Now, appliqué the inner curve. NOTE: It will be necessary to clip the curve at times; see instructions in Stitches page 32. Set your work down on a flat surface often and smooth it to prevent puckering.

5. Cut the motifs from a floral fabric leaving a ³⁄₁₆″ seam allowance around them. I overlapped several different motifs to achieve the arrangement on the Broderie Perse block in the *Heart Sampler Quilt.* Arrange and pin in place several fabric motifs.

6. Appliqué using the tack stitch or buttonhole stitch.

7. Press the completed block. See Pressing page 128.

SHADOW HEART BLOCK

1. Follow steps 1 and 2 in the *Heart Sampler Quilt* instructions.

2. Prepare fabric motif shapes (you may want to first join the fabric to fusible interfacing for body). See About Templates page 20. NOTE: Do *not* add seam allowance.

3. Center the block of ground fabric right side up on the pattern for the placement of fabric motif shapes. Use a small *dab* of fabric glue stick under each fabric motif shape to adhere it to the ground fabric. NOTE: The motif shapes will just touch one another. Do *not* overlap the shapes.

4. Place the voile overlay on top of the prepared ground block. Baste with large running stitches around the entire design.

5. Using thread the color of the motif, start at no. 1 on the outer curve of the heart and appliqué using the running stitch. Stitch through the three layers of fabric, just inside the cut edge of the motif.

6. Continue around the heart, down the calyx of the flower, and up around the inner curve of the heart ending at no. 1.

7. Appliqué each motif in this manner.

8. Trim the edge of the voile to within ¼″ of the outside of the heart motif. Turn under a small seam allowance and, with white thread, appliqué right next to the edge of the motif using the running stitch.

9. Press the block. See Pressing page 128.

HAWAIIAN HEART BLOCK

1. Follow steps 1 and 2 in the *Heart Sampler Quilt* instructions.

2. Prepare the fabric motif adding a ³⁄₁₆″ seam allowance to only the outside of the heart. Inside the heart, trace the lines to be used for reverse appliqué following your template.

3. Make a cut in the center of the fabric motif for reverse appliqué. See page 25 for more information about reverse appliqué. NOTE: You *need* a snip to put the scissors into at the time you cut away to appliqué.

4. Center the block of ground fabric right side up on the pattern. Pin the fabric heart motif in place and baste. NOTE: Do not baste inside the line drawn for reverse appliqué.

5. Begin reverse appliqué, placing tiny pointed scissors into the center snip and cutting on the drawn line. Using the round wooden toothpick, turn under ⅛″ to ³⁄₁₆″ seam allowance. Clip where necessary to achieve smooth curves and dips.

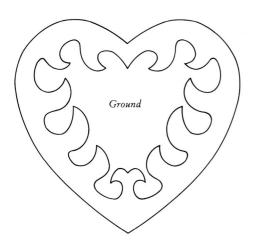

6. Turn under seam allowance on the outside edge of the heart shape. Appliqué using the tack stitch.

7. Press the completed block. See Pressing page 128.

BUTTONHOLE STITCH HEART BLOCK

1. Follow steps 1, 2, and 3 in the *Heart Sampler Quilt* instructions.

2. Center the block of ground fabric right side up on the pattern and pin heart motif 1 in place.

3. Using a round wooden toothpick, turn under ³⁄₁₆″ seam allowance on an outer curve of the heart shape. With the seam allowance folded under, appliqué using the buttonhole stitch. NOTE: Choose threads of contrasting colors and keep the stitches even. You want them to be seen as a decorative addition to the block.

4. Continue the appliqué, first placing and stitching heart 2 and then heart 3.

5. Press the completed block. See Pressing page 128.

Pa ndau Snailhouses Heart Block

In this block, the off-white ground fabric will function as an overlay and will be cut away and reverse appliquéd to reveal a darker underlay. See page 25 for basic reverse appliqué instructions.

1. Follow step 1 in the *Heart Sampler Quilt* instructions.

2. Center the overlay fabric right side up on the pattern, and trace the design with a sharp lead pencil. NOTE: You will be able to see the design through the off-white ground fabric.

3. With sharp pointed scissors, make a snip in the center of each row that will be cut away to reveal the lower color. NOTE: Pattern has lines (—) indicating snips.

4. Center the overlay fabric right side up on the right side of the dark underlay. Using small running stitches, baste down the center of every row that has not been snipped and around the entire outside edge of the block.

5. Reverse appliqué the coiled snailhouses, starting at no. 1. Place tiny sharp scissors into the snip and cut down the center of the row an inch at a time. Using a round wooden toothpick, turn under seam allowance. Finger press. Using the tack stitch, appliqué one side of the cut line. Then go back and do the same to the other side of the cut line. NOTE: I place the work down on a flat surface to start. It is easier to use the toothpick and finger press when you have both hands free.

6. Complete one snailhouse. Then start at no. 1 again to stitch the other snailhouse.

7. Now begin the outer heart at no. 2 and reverse appliqué, clipping curves as necessary. Stitch the inner and outer edges of the heart frame.

8. Place sharp pointed scissors into the snip of one cross. Cut both directions on the drawn line and stitch. NOTE: Your basting stitches will hold the fabric in place for you.

9. Remove all basting threads. Press the completed block. See Pressing page 128.

Stained Glass Heart Block

1. Follow steps 1 and 2 in the *Heart Sampler Quilt* instructions.

2. Prepare fabric shapes using one of the methods detailed in Essentials. NOTE: Do *not* add seam allowances. Cut shapes out on drawn line.

3. Center the block of ground fabric right side up on the pattern. Pin and baste the four window fabric shapes in place to the ground fabric.

4. Prepare bias tubing—cut bias 1″ wide for a finished bias tube of ¼″; see Bias Preparation page 23.

5. Measure the distance from no. 1 to no. 2 on the pattern. Add 1″ to the measurement, and cut the bias tube.

6. Place bias tube over the raw edges of the motifs, leaving a tail of ½″ at no. 1 and ½″ at no. 2. Pin only an inch or two at a time as you appliqué. NOTE: Do not pin *into* the bias tube, pin *across* it.

7. Starting at no. 1 and on the top edge of the bias tube, appliqué through the bias tube, fabric motif, and ground fabric using the tack or the ladder stitch. Hold the bias tube down with your left hand.

8. Now, appliqué the lower edge of the bias tube. As you reach the point of the motif it will be necessary to take a small tuck or pleat to turn the corner. Finger press in place and continue the appliqué.

9. Begin pinning bias tube in place at no. 3. NOTE: Pin only an inch or so at a time as you appliqué.

10. Starting at no. 3 and on the top edge of the bias tube, stitch the tube in place, looping around the outside of the heart and ending at no. 4. NOTE: Trim the tails of the bias tube as you come to them and cover the raw edges.

11. Now start at no. 4 and appliqué the remaining bias edge.

12. Press the completed block (see Pressing page 128).

To Finish Your Heart Sampler Quilt Top

You are now ready to set your blocks together and add the border. Return to the *Heart Sampler Quilt* instructions page 37 and proceed.

Chapter 4

~

APPLIQUÉING WITH
DECORATIVE STITCHES

SOMETIMES AN APPLIQUÉD MOTIF NEEDS ADDITIONAL EMPHASIS. THE FABRIC is just not enough. When that happens you might consider adding stitchery to your design. Embroidery stitches—running, buttonhole, chain, outline, or colonial knots—add to the design. The *Sunbonnet Sue* and *Butterfly* quilts of the 1920s and 1930s are appliquéd with the running stitch and the buttonhole stitch. The molas from the San Blas Islands and the Pa ndau appliquéd by the Hmong women are decorated with colonial knots and running stitches. Chain stitches, outline stitches, and colonial knots embellish the Album quilts of the midnineteenth century.

In this chapter, the *Sunbonnet Sue Quilt* is appliquéd with black floss, using the running stitch. The *Butterfly Quilt* is appliquéd with black floss, using the buttonhole stitch. The appliqué of the *Cradle Coverlet* is done in the buttonhole stitch with sewing thread. In all of these quilts, the decorative stitch is the actual stitch used to apply the motif to the ground fabric, so the stitch is both beautiful and necessary to the appliqué technique. In Broderie Perse and some of the nineteenth-century antique quilts, the buttonhole stitch is an option as the appliqué stitch.

SUNBONNET SUE QUILT

Sunbonnet Sue has been around a long time. She's a beloved old favorite to some and shunned by others, but we have given her a new look in this quilt. I hope you love the new homespuns, plaids, and stripes as much as we do. Shirley Weagant has put together a *Sunbonnet Sue* charm quilt using a different stripe and plaid in each block. Charm quilts, with no fabrics used more than once in a quilt, offer you the opportunity to use your scraps. You can use plaids and stripes as we have, or you can make a more traditional *Sunbonnet Sue,* using prints and solids. Your choice of fabrics makes your quilt unique. Although it takes a bit of effort to coordinate if you use two prints or a stripe and plaid, the effect will please you. If you use two prints, vary their pattern sizes. If you're using plaids and stripes, the colors will be the determining factor in achieving your overall effect.

Sunbonnet Sue Quilt, *appliquéd and quilted by Shirley Weagant*

SUNBONNET SUE QUILT

STITCHING TECHNIQUE	Running
SETTING	Diagonal set with sashing
FABRIC SUGGESTIONS	
Ground and backing	Light print or solid
Dress, sleeve, and bonnet band	Variety of plaids or variety of large or medium prints
Bonnet and pocket	Variety of stripes or variety of medium or small prints
Shoe	Black solid
Sashing and border	Plaid, print, or solid
Binding	Same fabric as sashing and border or plaid, print, or solid

	CRIB/WALL	TWIN	DOUBLE/QUEEN
FINISHED SIZE	42″×59″	75″×92″	92″×92″
BLOCKS SET	2×3	4×5	5×5
10″×10″ BLOCKS	8	32	41

YARDAGE

	CRIB/WALL	TWIN	DOUBLE/QUEEN
GROUND			
Appliqué blocks, side triangles, and corner triangles	1½	3¾	4¾
MOTIFS			
Dress, sleeve, and band (8″×8″ scraps—approx.)	½	1½	2
Bonnet and pocket (6″×6″ scraps—approx.)	⅓	1	1¼
SHOE	⅛	¼	¼
SASHING AND BORDER	1¾	2½	3½
BACKING	1¾	5½	7¾
BATTING	46″×63″	79″×96″	96″×96″
BINDING	½	⅝	¾
EMBROIDERY FLOSS (BLACK)	2 skeins	7 skeins	9 skeins

CUTTING

	CRIB/WALL	TWIN	DOUBLE/QUEEN
GROUND			
Appliqué blocks 12″×12″	8	32	41
Side triangles 13″×13″×18¼″	6	14	16
Corner triangles 11″×11″×15½″	4	4	4
MOTIFS			
Dress, sleeve, bonnet, bonnet band, shoe, and pocket	8 each	32 each	41 each
SASHING WIDTH	2½″	2½″	2½″
BORDER WIDTH	3″	3″	3″
BACKING LENGTHS	1	2	3
BINDING WIDTH	1½″	1½″	1½″

1. Prepare large pattern as your guide. See Pattern Preparation on page 20. Patterns are in the back of the book.

2. Next, make your motif templates: bonnet (one piece), bonnet band, dress, sleeve, pocket, shoe. Choose a method from About Templates page 20.

3. Prepare fabric motifs using one of the methods detailed in Essentials. Remember to add ³⁄₁₆″ seam allowance to your motif pieces as you cut.

4. Pin bonnet band onto bonnet using the large pattern as a guide for placement.

5. Turn under seam allowance and appliqué using running stitch.

6. Pin sleeve and pocket onto dress using the pattern guide for placement. Cover the straight raw edge of the sleeve with pocket. Appliqué in place using the running stitch.

7. Center ground fabric right side up on pattern guide and pin dress, bonnet, and shoe in place.

8. Using a round wooden toothpick, turn under seam allowance on dress front starting at the bonnet. Finger press.

9. With the seam allowance folded under, appliqué using the running stitch. Continue around the entire dress. NOTE: Fold under the seam allowance on the sides of the shoe as you appliqué the dress.

10. Next, fold under the seam allowance and appliqué using the running stitch around the shoe and the bonnet. Trim the block to 10½″ × 10½″.

11. Complete all blocks following steps 4–10.

To finish the quilt, see Finishing, chapter 13, for instructions on pressing, setting blocks together (see Diagonal Set with Sashing page 131), adding mitred borders, preparing batting, preparing backing, assembling the three layers, quilting, and binding.

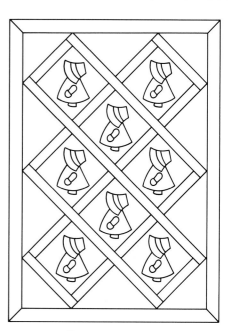

PLACEMENT DIAGRAM

Are they butterflies? Or are they moths? I have had the antique blocks in this quilt for several years just resting happily among the many blocks and quilt tops I have in my collection. When I began planning this book I wanted you to have several buttonhole stitch projects, and I remembered this almost funky set of blocks. When I took them out of the box they suddenly seemed exciting. Because each butterfly is a different fabric, they make a lovely charm quilt. They're made from fabrics from the 1930s ranging in scale of prints (small, medium, large) and designs (geometric, floral, and polka dot). They created a delightful color wheel effect including red, purple, brown, blue, green, and orange—practically every imaginable color. But I still don't know if they're butterflies or moths.

This quilt will be just as exciting in today's fabrics if you use as many different prints as you have blocks. Use your scraps. Surprisingly, the fabrics fit together and are as eye appealing as many quilts that have been carefully color coordinated. Experiment with lots of different colors and patterns. You will become an expert!

Butterfly Quilt, *antique blocks appliquéd by unknown quilter and quilted by Shirley Weagant*

BUTTERFLY QUILT

STITCHING TECHNIQUES	Buttonhole, outline, colonial knot
SETTING	Diagonal set
FABRIC SUGGESTIONS	
Ground and backing	Light solid
Motifs	Variety of large, medium, and small prints
Binding	Print or solid to complement dominant color of blocks

	LAP	DOUBLE/QUEEN	KING
FINISHED SIZE	63″ × 76″	88″ × 101″	101″ × 101″
BLOCKS SET	5 × 6	7 × 8	8 × 8
9″ × 9″ BLOCKS	50	98	113

YARDAGE

	LAP	DOUBLE/QUEEN	KING
GROUND	4½	7½	8½
MOTIFS			
Scraps to total	3½	6¼	7¼
BACKING	5	9	9
BATTING	67″ × 80″	92″ × 105″	105″ × 105″
BINDING	½	¾	¾
EMBROIDERY FLOSS (BLACK)	5 skeins	9 skeins	11 skeins

CUTTING

	LAP	DOUBLE/QUEEN	KING
GROUND			
Blocks 11″ × 11″	50	98	113
Side triangles 10″ × 10″ × 14″	18	26	28
Corner triangles 7½″ × 7½″ × 10½″	4	4	4
MOTIFS	50	98	113
BACKING LENGTHS	2	3	3
BINDING WIDTH	1½″	1½″	1½″

1. Prepare a pattern as your guide. See Pattern Preparation page 20. See Template Patterns in the back of the book.

2. Prepare the butterfly motif template. Choose a method from About Templates page 20.

3. Prepare fabric motifs using one of the methods detailed in Essentials. Make sure you add ³⁄₁₆″ seam allowance as you cut.

4. Using the pattern as a guide, center butterfly motif diagonally on ground fabric; pin in place with sequin pins.

5. Turn under seam allowance. With one 2-ply strand of floss, appliqué the motif using the buttonhole stitch. NOTE: Make sure your stitches are even, or your butterfly will end up looking like the one pictured here.

6. With yellow or white dressmaker's carbon, trace embroidery lines onto butterfly and ground fabrics.

7. Embroider with one 2-ply strand of floss; outline stitch the lines and make colonial knots for eyes. Trim block to 9½″ × 9½″.

8. Follow steps 4–7 until all blocks are complete.

To finish this quilt, see Finishing, chapter 13, for instructions on pressing completed blocks, setting blocks together (see Diagonal Set page 130), preparing batting, preparing backing, assembling three layers, quilting, and binding.

SUMMER CRADLE COVERLET OR TABLE TOPPER

Do you love fine linens as much as I do? As a young bride I was hostess at many bridge luncheons, and we always covered the tables with lovely linens. Some were embroidered, some were edged with lace, and some were appliqué and embroidery combined. The latter, my favorites, were made in China with delicate embroidery, soft solid-colored fabrics, and exquisite buttonhole stitches.

It occurred to me that not too many people have bridge luncheons anymore. So I have designed this lovely, dainty appliqué that you may also use as a summer cradle coverlet for a beautiful baby. My friend Elizabeth Derivan enjoyed stitching this coverlet.

Summer Cradle Coverlet, *appliquéd by Elizabeth Derivan*

SUMMER CRADLE COVERLET OR TABLE TOPPER

STITCHING TECHNIQUES	Buttonhole, chain, outline, ladder
SETTING	Whole cloth
FABRIC SUGGESTIONS	*All solids*
Ground and backing	Off-white
Leaf motifs	Medium green and dark green
Flower motifs	Light, medium, and dark shades of one or more of the following: pink, purple, peach, blue, yellow
FINISHED SIZE	30″ × 30″

YARDAGE

GROUND AND BACKING	2
MOTIFS	
Leaves	¼ each green: medium, dark
Flowers	¼ each pink: light, medium, dark; blue: light, medium, dark
	⅛ each purple: light, medium, dark; peach: light, medium, dark; scraps of yellow: light, dark
THREAD	1 spool size 60, machine embroidery, off-white to match ground fabric; 1 skein each, light and dark green floss; 1 ball size 5 perle cotton, medium green

CUTTING

GROUND AND BACKING	
34″ × 34″	2
LEAVES	
Shape A—medium green	4
Shape B—dark green	4
Shape C—dark green	4
FLOWERS	
Shape 1, light	4 each, blue, pink, peach, purple, yellow
Shape 2, medium	4 each, blue, pink, peach, purple, yellow
Shape 3, dark	4 each, blue, pink, peach, purple, yellow
Shape 4, light	4 each, blue, purple
Shape 5, medium	4 each, blue, purple
Shape 6, dark	4 each, blue, purple

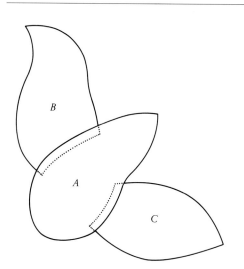

DIAGRAM 1

1. Prepare one large pattern as your guide. See Pattern Preparation page 20. NOTE: All four corners are the same. See Template Patterns in the back of the book.

2. Center the ground fabric, right side up, on your pattern guide, and mark all stems, vines, and tiny leaves lightly with a no. 2½ lead pencil. The pencil lines will be embroidered in chain and outline stitches.

3. Center backing fabric, wrong side up, on pattern and mark the outside edge. Do not cut. *Mark only.*

4. Prepare your motif templates for all flower petals and large leaves. See About Templates page 20.

5. Prepare fabric shapes using one of the methods detailed in Essentials. NOTE: Add ³⁄₁₆" seam allowance as you cut out each piece.

6. With dressmaker's carbon, trace embroidery lines onto leaf shapes.

7. Pin 3 leaves in a corner with sequin pins, using the large pattern as your guide for placement. The vines and stems drawn on the ground fabric will aid in perfect placement. REMEMBER: Leaf A is placed on top of leaves B and C. All the raw edges under leaf A should be flat. *(See diagram 1).*

8. Start leaf C at the edge under leaf A; turn under ³⁄₁₆" seam allowance and appliqué in place using a very fine buttonhole stitch. NOTE: Size 60 off-white machine embroidery thread is used on all appliqué. Take tiny stitches (¹⁄₁₆") barely catching the edge of the motif.

9. Continue the appliqué with leaf B and end with leaf A.

10. Pin a large blue flower in place with sequin pins, using the large pattern as guide for placement. REMEMBER: The stems and leaves drawn on the ground fabric will aid in placement.

11. Start blue flower petal 1 at the edge under petal 2. Turn under ³⁄₁₆" seam allowance and appliqué using a very fine buttonhole stitch.

12. Continue appliqué with petal 2 and finally petal 3.

13. The balance of the flowers will be appliquéd as above. SUGGESTION: Do the larger flowers first, medium flowers next, and smallest flowers last. You will have better control of the tiny pieces of fabric that way.

14. Repeat steps 7–13 in each corner until all 4 corners are completed.

15. With a 2-ply strand of dark green floss embroider all stems and vines using the chain stitch.

16. With a 1-ply strand of dark green floss embroider all small leaves using the outline stitch.

17. With a 1-ply strand of light green floss embroider all veins in appliquéd leaves using the outline stitch.

18. Press following instructions. See Finishing page 128.

19. With right sides together, pin quilt top to backing. Stitch together following drawn line on backing fabric. Leave an 8" opening. Trim seam allowance to ¼" and turn. Handstitch the opening.

20. Press following instructions. See Finishing page 128. As you press, pull the edges of the *Summer Cradle Coverlet* so top and back are even.

21. Finish the edge of the *Summer Cradle Coverlet* with size 5 perle cotton in a matching green using ¼" buttonhole stitches.

Chapter 5

~

STAINED GLASS AND CELTIC APPLIQUÉ

Bias tubes are used in the appliqué styles in this chapter. Stained glass uses a black bias tube that simulates the lead seams of genuine stained-glass windows. In most stained glass instructions, the bias tube is ¼" wide. I find it much easier to maneuver a ³⁄₁₆" bias tube around curves and points, and the narrower bias is more pleasing to the eye when the fabric motif pieces are small. The *Della Robia Wreath Quilt* is appliquéd with a black ³⁄₁₆" bias tube.

The Celtic knot is a study in complex curves. We'll use a bias tube at least ¼" wide in this complicated appliqué design. I have given a new dimension to the Celtic style by stitching two fabrics side by side to be used in the bias tube. As the bias wanders through the design, the two fabrics change sides, adding dimension and interest to the design.

When you have completed the two projects in this chapter you will have the expertise to attempt others, perhaps your own designs. Good luck!

Della Robia Wreath Quilt

I love everything about Christmas. Watching the crowds in the shopping malls, planning gifts for friends and loved ones, spending the inevitable late nights trying to finish all the planned projects, listening to the carols sung over and over again, decorating the house and the "prettiest tree we've ever had" with holiday treasures—this all gives me great pleasure. Mmm, the soft lights of the tree, a cup of hot spiced cider—I could sit forever, dreaming in front of a crackling fire!

Since I'm in love with Christmas, it seemed only proper to have a tiny bit of Christmas in this book. This *Della Robia Wreath Quilt* filled with fruit was one of those "middle of the night" inspirations. I finished the sketches in mere minutes. The full-size design was a delight to draw. The bright primary-colored fabrics were sitting on my shelves just waiting to be chosen.

Of course, these colors aren't just for Christmas. You may hang this wreath year round.

My friend Linda Aiken agreed to do the appliqué. Linda also designed the border and added the eight bars from the wreath to the border. They're perfect finishing touches.

This design does not follow the stained glass window composition absolutely—the lead channels (bias tubes) do not continue to the outside edges (the borders). And many of the shapes float—impossible to attain in glass but not difficult in fabric. I have taken artistic license. Fabric and glass aren't the same, but they are kindred spirits!

In the late 1970s and early 1980s, I collected a group of fabrics that had a batik look. Many shades of the same color, sometimes streaked very dark and sometimes very light, appeared within a half-yard length of fabric: reds, yellows, blues, greens, purples, and more. As you choose the fabrics for your wall quilt, look for bright primary colors, either solids or with almost invisible designs. You may want to choose fabrics with a mottled or variegated appearance. Both those and hand-dyed fabrics create the almost perfect resemblance to glass. Perhaps you have some of the fabrics from the late 1970s in your stash or other fabrics that will be just right.

You won't be able to put this work down once you have started. Each finished shape invites you to hurry to do another and another just to see how it looks! It's easy, fun, and addictive!

Della Robia Wreath Quilt, *appliquéd and quilted by Linda Aiken*

DELLA ROBIA WREATH QUILT

STITCHING TECHNIQUES	Tack, ladder
FABRIC SUGGESTIONS	*Inconspicuous prints or solids*
Ground and backing	Off-white
MOTIFS	
Leaves	Greens: light, medium, dark
Pears	Yellow
Orange	Orange
Plums	Deep blues
Peaches	Tangerine, red-orange
Grapes	Purples
Apples	Red
Border	Various scraps of motifs
Bias tube	Black
FINISHED SIZE	25″ × 25″

YARDAGE

GROUND AND BACKING	1¾
MOTIFS	
Leaves	⅛ each, light, medium, dark
Pears	⅙ each, 2 different
Orange	⅛
Plums	⅛ each, 3 different
Peaches	⅛ each, 2 different
Grapes	⅛ each, 4 different
Apples	⅛ each, 2 different
BIAS TUBE (³⁄₁₆″)	¾
BATTING	29″ × 29″

CUTTING

GROUND AND BACKING		
29″ × 29″	2	
MOTIFS		
Leaves	1 each of patterns 1–7, 11, 15, 16, 18, 22, 23, 25–27, 30, 31, 33, 35, 38–46, 49, 59	
Pears	1 each of patterns 17, 36, 60	
Orange	1 of pattern 28	
Plums	1 each of patterns 8, 9, 10, 12, 13, 14, 29, 32, 34, 37	
Peaches	1 each of patterns 20, 24, 47, 48	
Grapes	1 each of patterns 50–58	
Apples	1 each of patterns 19, 21	
BIAS TUBE	⅞″	
BORDER		
Corners 2½″ × 2½″	4	
Rectangles 2½″ ×	Choose lengths to fit your taste and finished piece	
BINDING WIDTH	1½″	

CONSTRUCTION

1. Prepare a large pattern as a guide. See Pattern Preparation page 20. See Template Patterns in the back of the book.

2. Prepare the templates. Be sure to number each one. See About Templates page 20.

3. Prepare fabric shapes using one of the methods detailed in Essentials. NOTE: Do *not* add seam allowance. Cut out shapes on drawn lines.

4. Prepare ³⁄₁₆″ bias tube (cut ⅞″ bias strips). See Bias Preparation page 23.

5. On the right side of ground fabric draw a straight line 4½″ from all 4 sides. You will have a 20″ drawn square. NOTE: Drawn lines on the pattern will be covered by bias tubes on the worked piece.

PLACEMENT DIAGRAM

6. With ground fabric on pattern for placement, pin leaf motif no. 1 for appliqué.

7. Measure the distance around motif to be appliquéd. Cut bias tube adding 1″ to measurement. *(See diagram 1.)* NOTE: On all circles add 2″ to the measurement. Circles seem to eat up the bias tube.

8. With half of the bias tube on motif fabric and half on ground fabric, begin pinning in place. Only pin an inch or two at a time. *(See diagram 2.)* NOTE: Place the bulky side of the bias tube on the motif fabric. Do not pin *into* the bias tube. Pin *across* it—pinning into the ground fabric and into the motif fabric.

9. Starting at the inner fold of the bias tube and at the edge of the motif fabric, appliqué through motif and ground fabric using either the tack or ladder stitch.

10. As you reach the point of the motif it will be necessary to take a small tuck or pleat to turn the corner. Finger press in place and continue the appliqué. *(See diagram 3.)* NOTE: To keep the motif flat when appliquéing the

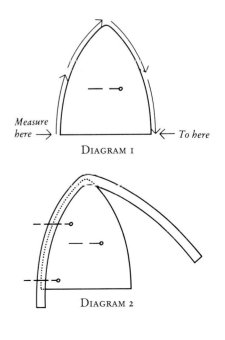

Measure here → ← *To here*

DIAGRAM 1

DIAGRAM 2

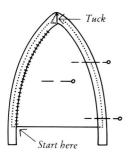

DIAGRAM 3

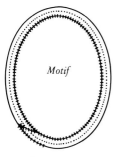

DIAGRAM 4

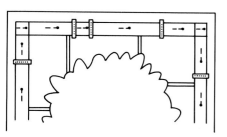

DIAGRAM 5

inner fold of the bias tube, reach your needle out with a scooping motion to grab the motif fabric and pull it toward the bias tube.

11. Now appliqué the outer fold of the bias tube. The point is perfect (no more tucking is necessary). NOTE: Do *not* trim ends of bias tube until they are covered by adjoining motifs.

12. With ground fabric on pattern for placement, pin next motif.

13. Repeat steps 7–12, working with the motifs in numerical order until all motifs have been appliquéd. As you appliqué, watch for the following things:

- Motif no. 2: Leave ½″ open on outer fold of bias tube to slide bar no. 61 under.
- Motif no. 4: Leave ½″ open on outer fold of bias tube to slide bar no. 62 under.
- Motif no. 24: Leave ½″ open on outer fold of the bias tube to slide bar no. 63 under.
- Motif no. 25: Leave ½″ open on outer fold of the bias tube to slide bar no. 64 under.
- Motif no. 37: As you finish the appliqué of the inner fold of the bias tube, stitch diagonally across—to overlap the trimmed raw edge of the beginning of the tube. Continue by appliquéing the outer fold of the bias tube. Trim and tuck in the raw end as you appliqué. *(See diagram 4.)*
- Motif no. 40: Leave ½″ open on outer fold of the bias tube to slide bar no. 66 under.
- Motif no. 42: Leave outer fold of the bias tube unstitched where it covers motif no. 60 until motif no. 60 is appliquéd.
- Motif no. 46: Leave ½″ open on outer fold of the bias tube to slide bar no. 67 under.
- Motif no. 50: Leave ½″ open on outer fold of the bias tube to slide bar no. 65 under.
- Motif no. 60: Leave ½″ open on outer fold of the bias tube to slide bar no. 68 under.

14. Prepare bars (motif nos. 61–68) by measuring from the motif to the drawn line. Add 1″ to each measurement and cut bias tube. Tuck the bar into the ½″ opening in the motif. Stitch toward the drawn line. Trim if necessary.

15. Pin corner motifs A, B, C, and D to ground fabric just outside the drawn line.

16. To form the border, measure various fabric rectangles 2½″ × different lengths. You choose. Pin them in place, adjacent to and touching one another, around the outside of the drawn line.

17. Appliqué bias tubes over all butted fabric except the corners. *(See diagram 5.)*

18. Appliqué bias tube down the inside edges of the border on the drawn line, covering the edges of the corner squares as well.

To finish the quilt, see Finishing, chapter 13, for instructions on pressing the completed top, preparing the backing, preparing the batting, assembling the three layers, quilting, and binding.

CELTIC APPLIQUÉ WALL QUILT/TABLE RUNNER

In 1980 Philomena Wiechec published *Celtic Quilt Designs,* a book filled with designs inspired by authentic Celtic knots perfect for bias appliqué. These intricate designs not only captivate anyone who loves appliqué, but they also provide a challenge. The over and under, in and out, up and down reminds me of some of the mazes my grandchildren enjoy. The end result is delicate and beautiful.

With the help of two friends, Ann Bevilockway and Linda Aiken, I have designed a table runner or wall quilt just for you. Ann brought *Knots: Useful & Ornamental* (published in 1924) by George Russell Shaw to our designing session. One section of *Knots* is devoted to Celtic knots. The design you see here was among several sketches in that section.

I knew the fabric choices were important to the final look. As I considered this, I came upon the idea of stitching two fabrics together, side by side, to make the bias tube. I consulted Linda, who was doing the appliqué. She agreed it would be interesting, different—and maybe even exceptional.

When the appliqué was finished it looked exactly as we had envisioned it. The quilting added to the beauty of the quilt. Linda says it is not difficult if you just pay attention to the overs and unders!

Celtic Appliqué Wall Quilt, *appliquéd by Linda Aiken and quilted by Lori Heikkila*

CELTIC APPLIQUÉ WALL QUILT/TABLE RUNNER

STITCHING TECHNIQUES	Tack, ladder
FABRIC SUGGESTIONS	*Prints or solids*
Ground	White
Bias tube	Medium green; dark green
Borders	Same greens as bias
Backing	White
Binding	Same dark green
FINISHED SIZE	18″ × 54″

YARDAGE

GROUND AND BACKING	1⅔
BIAS TUBE, BORDERS, AND BINDING	1⅔ each color
BATTING	22″ × 58″

CUTTING

GROUND	16″ × 52″
BIAS TUBE (¾″)	3½ yds., each print
BORDER WIDTHS	
Inside border	Dark print: 2—1″ × 17″, 2—1″ × 53″
Outside border	Medium print: 2—2″ × 20″, 2—2″ × 56″
BACKING	22″ × 58″
BINDING WIDTH	1½″ wide, dark green print

CONSTRUCTION

1. Prepare a large pattern as your guide. See Pattern Preparation page 20. See also Template Patterns at the back of the book.

2. Cut your ground fabric.

3. Cut the border fabric according to Cutting. NOTE: Cut the borders before preparing bias tube to avoid having to piece borders later.

4. Use the remaining fabric to create bias tubes. Cut bias strips ¾″ wide of each fabric. Sew these with right sides together using ¼″ seam allowance. Press seam open. Use this resulting strip to create bias tube with two shades of green. See Bias Preparation page 23. You will need a total of 3½ yds. of bias tube.

5. Center ground fabric, right side up, on pattern guide and mark all lines with a pencil. NOTE: The pencil lines will guide your placement of the bias tube.

6. As you appliqué, you may want to roll up the ground fabric you aren't working with and pin it to keep it out of the way.

7. Start at no. 1 on the diagram. Leaving a ½″ tail, pin two or three inches of bias tube to ground fabric following drawn lines. *(See diagram 7.)*

8. Starting on the inner fold of the bias tube, appliqué through the bias tube and the ground fabric using the tack or ladder stitch.

9. As you appliqué, the bias tubes will eventually cross. If the tube you are appliquéing is on top in the design, leave ¾″ open so you can slide the bottom tube through as you complete the design. You will appliqué these openings when you cross under them. NOTE: If a bias tube is too short, do not piece it. Cut it at an "under" section and start another so the ends will be covered by an "over."

10. When you reach the end at no. 1, leave a ½″ tail. You will cut these when they are covered by other bias tubes. Now appliqué the outer curve of the bias tube.

11. When you have completed loop no. 1, begin at no. 2 on the diagram. When loop no. 2 is completed, begin at no. 3. Trim appliquéd piece to 14½″ × 50½″, centering the design.

To finish the quilt, see Finishing, chapter 13, for instructions on adding mitred corner borders, pressing the completed quilt top, preparing batting, preparing backing, assembling the three layers, quilting, and binding.

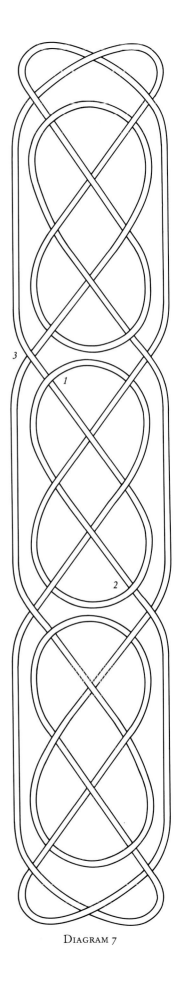

DIAGRAM 7

Chapter 6

~

HAWAIIAN APPLIQUÉ

KAPA IS THE HAWAIIAN WORD FOR QUILT. "KA-PA, KA-PA—YOU MUST PRO-
nounce it correctly," Wailani Johansen, a well-known Hawaiian quilter,
reminded us. (It rhymes with ha, ha.) We were a classroom full of novice
quilters hoping to become expert in the art of Hawaiian quilting. On that day
I fell in love with Hawaiian quilting and in love with Wailani. This gentle, soft-
spoken teacher reminded each of us that "everything beautiful requires a little
effort and patience."

When you look at a Hawaiian quilt with an intricate *kapalau* (appliqué
design), it becomes obvious that Wailani speaks the truth. Many of the large
quilts take a year or perhaps two to complete. But "beautiful" seems an
understatement when describing them.

Traditionally, these quilts combine two colors—a dark color for the
appliqué design and a light color for the background. Turkey red and white
are typical of the quilts made in the late nineteenth and early twentieth
centuries. The Hawaiian quilt is a unique combination of a "snowflake"
design cut from one piece of fabric, appliquéd onto a ground fabric, and then
quilted, following the outline of the design in waves to the edge of the quilt.

There are two quilts to choose from in this chapter, one based on a
traditional design, and one antique.

Hawaiian Sampler Quilt, *appliquéd by Annette Mahon and quilted by Anna Christner*

Hawaiian Sampler Quilt

Remember, *kapa* is the Hawaiian word for quilt. And *pohopoho* is the word for patchwork. *Kapa pohopoho* is a quilt with sashings and borders. This sampler quilt of paper-cut designs is our *kapa pohopoho*. To be more correct, we should call it our *houli kapa pohopoho*, a mainland sampler quilt!

Traditional Hawaiian paper-cut designs are inspired by Hawaii's beautiful trees and flowers. I followed this example. The pineapple, breadfruit, anthurium, and plumeria designs in this sampler are original but inspired by Hawaiian quilts.

I began creating the patterns by folding four squares of paper into quarters and then along the bias line. Then I drew the designs and cut them out. When I unfolded the paper, sometimes the designs were just right. Other times I needed to make some adjustments. Next, I worked with full-size paper: folded it, drew the design, and cut out the design. It is not difficult. Give it a try!

I took these designs one step beyond their traditional origins as I put them into fabric. Two of the blocks are worked in the traditional solid turkey red. And two are in a marvelous batik fabric with stars covering a ground that radiates with shades of gold, blue, red, and orange. The sashing is a bright solid gold, and the border repeats the batik. I just love it. I hope you do, too!

Arizona quiltmaker Annette Mahon loves Hawaii, the Hawaiian culture, and Hawaiian quilts. Annette does beautiful appliqué and she does it quickly. The appliqué of this wall quilt took only a few weeks. It is the hand quilting that takes longer!

If you repeat the blocks, you can make a twin, double/queen, or king size quilt. Fabric requirements and measurements are included. You choose which blocks and where to place them.

HAWAIIAN SAMPLER QUILT

STITCHING TECHNIQUES	Tack, ladder
SETTING	Straight set with sashing
FABRIC SUGGESTIONS	
Ground	Light solid
Motifs	Dark solid, print
Sashing	Solid
Border	Print, as motif
Backing	Light solid
Binding	Print, as motif and border

	WALL	TWIN	DOUBLE/QUEEN	KING
FINISHED SIZE	51″×51″	59″×80″	80″×101″	101″×101″
BLOCKS SET	2×2	2×3	3×4	4×4
18″×18″ NUMBER BLOCKS	4	6	12	16

YARDAGE

	WALL	TWIN	DOUBLE/QUEEN	KING
GROUND	1¼	1¾	3½	4½
MOTIF				
Solid	½	1	1½	2
Print	½	1	1½	2
SASHING	1	2	2¾	2¾
BORDER AND BINDING	1⅔	2½	3	3
BACKING	3¼	4¾	6	9
BATTING	55″×55″	63″×84″	84″×105″	105″×105″

CUTTING

	WALL	TWIN	DOUBLE/QUEEN	KING
GROUND				
20″×20″	4	6	12	16
MOTIFS				
18″×18″	4	6	12	16
SASHING WIDTH	2″	3½″	3½″	3½″
BORDER WIDTH	5½″	7½″	7½″	7½″
BACKING LENGTHS	2	2	2	3
BINDING WIDTH	1½″	1½″	1½″	1½″

CONSTRUCTION

1. Using butcher paper, prepare templates for the motifs. See Pattern Preparation page 20. See also patterns at the end of the book.

2. With right side out, fold a ground fabric into eighths as shown. Then, again with right side out, fold one motif fabric. Press to crease. (See diagram 1.) Set aside the ground fabric.

3. Place your template on the right side of the motif fabric with bias edge on bias folds and straight edge on straight folds. Pin into place and draw around the entire template with a pencil. (See diagram 2.)

4. Remove the pins and template. Then pin or baste the fabric layers together so they don't slip while you cut the shape. Cut on the drawn line. NOTE: You do not add a seam allowance as you cut.

5. Unfold motif. Center on ground fabric, matching all creases, and pin into place.

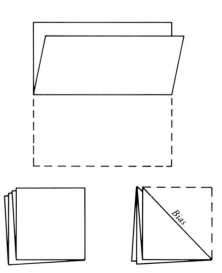

DIAGRAM I

Diagram 2

6. Baste through both layers, ½″ from cut edges, around entire motif. NOTE: No stitching line is drawn on the motif or on the ground fabric. You will turn under ⅛″ to 3/16″ seam allowance as you appliqué. Use your round wooden toothpick.

7. Starting on an outside curve, appliqué the motif in place using the tack or ladder stitch. NOTE: Two motifs have reverse appliqué sections. See page 25 for instructions.

    a. Pineapple: the centers of the four pineapples and the center of the motif.

    b. Anthurium: the centers of the four flowers and the center of the motif.

REMEMBER: Clip at the inner corners and curves. Stitches must be very tiny to make smooth curves and perfect points.

8. Continue in this manner until the entire block is appliquéd.

9. Press completed block. See Pressing page 128. Trim block to 18½″ × 18½″, centering the design.

10. Repeat steps 2–9 to complete all blocks.

To finish the quilt, see Finishing, chapter 13, for instructions on setting the blocks together (see Straight Set with Sashing page 129), adding mitred borders (see page 133), pressing the finished quilt top, preparing the batting, preparing the backing, assembling three layers, quilting (see Echo Quilting page 136), and binding.

ECHO QUILTING

HAWAIIAN QUILT

This quilt is a lovely example of Hawaiian quilting at its finest. The design is a challenge, with many points and inside curves. And, of course, the beauty comes from the complexity of the design. The border corners are unusual and reveal the gift of design the quiltmaker possessed.

The fabrics and colors are typical of the Hawaiian quilts—solid white ground, solid turkey red motif and binding. The quilting is also typical, with the lines a perfect half inch apart and undulating across the quilt in waves. The batting is relatively thick. I would not enjoy quilting such a batt, so I recommend a thinner one for your version.

My friend Elaine Wilhelm and I took a workshop with teacher Wailani Johansen many years ago. I made a pillow; Elaine started a king-size Hawaiian appliqué quilt. Every few months or so Elaine would stop by The Quilted Apple to visit and to report, "I have it almost all basted." Then, later, "I am appliquéing now." Finally, she reported, "I have it in the frame and I am quilting it." Several years passed before the beautiful quilt was finished and placed on her bed. It was her long-term quilt, and she enjoyed it during all the years of stitching.

This quilt is a long-term project, and if you're not a master appliquér when you begin, you'll become one in the process. Have fun!

HAWAIIAN QUILT

STITCHING TECHNIQUES	Tack, ladder
FABRIC SUGGESTIONS	*All solids*
Ground	Light
Motifs	Dark
Backing	Light
Binding	Dark
FINISHED SIZE	81″×88″

YARDAGE

GROUND	5½
MOTIFS	8
BACKING	5½
BATTING	85″×92″
BINDING	1

Hawaiian Quilt, *courtesy of The Ardis & Robert James Collection*

CUTTING

GROUND 85″ × 92″	1, pieced to size	
MOTIFS		
Center 60″ × 60″	1, pieced to size	
Corners 36″ × 36″	4	
BACKING LENGTHS	2	
BINDING WIDTH	1½″	

1. Using butcher paper, prepare templates for center and corner motifs. See About Templates page 20. Also see patterns at the end of the book. NOTE: These patterns are ½ size. Piece the ground fabric and center motif as you would backing. See Backing page 135.

2. With right side out, fold 85″×92″ ground fabric into eighths. *(See diagram 3.)* Press to crease. Repeat with the 60″×60″ center motif fabric. Set aside the ground fabric.

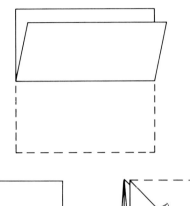

3. Place the template on the right side of center motif fabric with bias edge on bias folds and straight edge on straight folds. Pin into place and draw around entire template with a pencil. *(See diagram 4.)*

4. Remove the pins and template. Then pin or baste the fabric layers together so they won't slip while you cut the shape on the drawn line; cut and unfold the motif. Center the motif on the ground fabric matching all creases. NOTE: Motif is placed diagonally so that the bias folds of the motif match the straight folds of the ground fabric. Pin into place.

5. With right side out, fold one 36″×36″ corner motif fabric in half diagonally. Press to crease. *(See diagram 5.)* NOTE: Make one fold only—on the diagonal!

DIAGRAM 3

6. Place the template on the right side of the corner motif fabric with bias edge on bias fold. Pin into place and draw around the entire template with a pencil. *(See diagram 6.)*

7. Remove pins and template. Then pin or baste the fabric layers together so they won't slip while you cut the shape on the drawn line; cut and unfold the motif. Place on a corner of the ground fabric matching the diagonal creases. Pin into place. NOTE: As you place the motif on the ground fabric, be sure it's centered in the corner.

DIAGRAM 4

8. Repeat steps 5–7 with the three remaining corner motifs.

9. Baste through both layers, ½″ from cut edge, around the center and corner motifs. NOTE: No stitching line is drawn on the motif or the ground fabric. You will turn under ⅛″ to 3/16″ seam allowance as you appliqué. Use your round wooden toothpick. It makes it so easy!

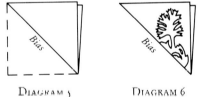

10. Starting on an outside curve, appliqué the motifs in place using the tack or ladder stitch. REMEMBER: Clip at inner corners and curves. Stitches must be very tiny to have smooth curves and perfect points.

DIAGRAM 5   DIAGRAM 6

To finish the quilt, see Finishing, chapter 13, for instructions on pressing the completed top, preparing the batting, preparing the backing, assembling three layers, quilting (see Echo Quilting page 136), and binding.

thei

curv

usir
curv

are

Poi
det

the
thre

YARDAGE

GROUND

Corner squares, triangles, and borders	8¼

STAR

	(See diagram 2 for arrangement)
Fabric no. 1	½
no. 2	⅔
no. 3	⅓
no. 4	½
no. 5	⅓
no. 6	⅓
no. 7	½
no. 8	½
no. 9	¼
MOTIFS	4
DOG'S TOOTH EDGE	1
SAWTOOTH EDGE AND BINDING	3
BACKING	9
BATTING	103″ × 103″

CUTTING

GROUND

Corner squares 18½″ × 18½″	4
Side Triangles 19″ × 19″ × 26¾″	4

STAR

Fabric no. 1	88 diamonds
no. 2	112 diamonds
no. 3	64 diamonds
no. 4	96 diamonds
no. 5	40 diamonds
no. 6	56 diamonds
no. 7	80 diamonds
no. 8	80 diamonds
no. 9	32 diamonds
APPLIQUÉ MOTIFS	Cut out with 3/16″ seam allowance
BORDER WIDTH	19″
DOG'S TOOTH EDGE	4 strips
SAWTOOTH EDGE	4 strips
BACKING LENGTHS	3
BINDING WIDTH	1½″

STAR

1. Make a templastic template of the diamond shape using the pattern on page 167. The pattern includes ¼″ seam allowance.

2. Cut the diamond shapes out of each fabric. Refer to Cutting for correct numbers. Carefully place the template on the straight grain of the fabric, following the arrow on the template pattern.

3. Arrange the diamond pieces for one point of the star in proper order. *(See diagram 2.)*

4. Stitch the diamonds in row 1 together using ¼″ seam.

5. Press seam allowances to one side. See Pressing page 128.

6. Stitch together the diamonds in row 2, and press the seam allowance in the opposite direction from row 1. Continue in this manner until all rows have been stitched and pressed.

7. With the right sides together, pin row 1 to row 2. Place your pins where the seams intersect. Stitch using a ¼″ seam. Continue in this manner to complete the point.

8. Now stitch the remaining points of the star following steps 3–7.

9. Press all seams to the outside point. *(See diagram 3.)*

10. Pin 2 points together, butting the seams. Sew from the center out. Press seams open.

11. Repeat step 10 until you have 4 pairs. Stitch 2 pairs together. Press seams open. Repeat. Now you have 2 halves of the star. *(See diagram 4.)*

12. Pin star halves together matching center seams. They will butt into one another because the seams are turned opposite directions. Stitch in place. Press last seams open.

13. Press entire star. Set aside.

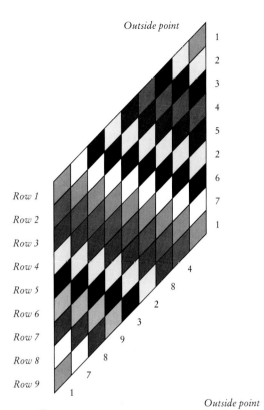

DIAGRAM 2

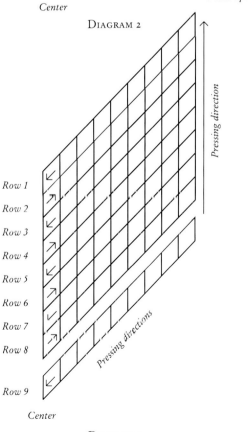

DIAGRAM 3

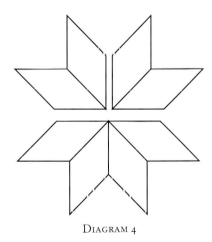

DIAGRAM 4

Shadow Appliqué Baby Quilt

Linda Aiken has added so much to this book, both in the actual appliqué and in design. This charming baby quilt is Linda's design and was inspired by a quilt made for our friend Diane Ebner. When Diane left California to live in Arizona, her quilting group, Mission Peak Quilters of Fremont, presented her with an adorable *Shadow Appliqué Baby Quilt,* our inspiration.

For the overlay fabric we have chosen a white voile, soft and pliable, perfect for a baby quilt. Three of the colored fabrics are solids. One of the fabrics is actually the reverse side of an almost invisible print. We chose this because the color was perfect. If you can't find the color you want, try choosing, as we did, from the wrong side of some of your fabrics.

Shadow Appliqué Baby Quilt, *appliquéd by Linda Aiken and quilted by Lori Heikkila*

SHADOW APPLIQUÉ BABY QUILT

STITCHING TECHNIQUES	Running, tack, ladder
SETTING	Diagonal set
FABRIC SUGGESTIONS	*Solids*
Ground	White cotton
Overlay	White voile
Motifs, sashing, beads, and binding	Pink, green, blue, and yellow
Backing	White cotton
FINISHED SIZE	43½″ × 43½″

YARDAGE

GROUND	2½
OVERLAY	2½
MOTIFS, SASHING, BEADS, AND BINDING	½ each color
FUSIBLE INTERFACING	2 (lightest weight)
BACKING	1½
BATTING	47½″ × 47½″
THREAD	1 spool of each, pink, blue, yellow, and green, size 50 or 60, 100 percent cotton

CUTTING

GROUND AND OVERLAY	
Center square 10½″ × 10½″	1
Rectangles 5½″ × 10½″	8
Small squares 5½″ × 5½″	4
Small triangles 6″ × 6″ × 8½″	8
Large triangles 8″ × 8″ × 11¼″	4
Border width	8″
MOTIFS	1 each (your color choice)
SASHING BEADS	
Small	32 each, pink, blue, yellow
Large	32 green
BACKING LENGTH	1
BINDING, 2½″ × 45″ STRIPS	3 each, pink, blue, yellow, green

CONSTRUCTION

1. Prepare butcher paper patterns for center square, eight rectangles, four small squares. See Cutting for measurements.

2. Make templastic template for sashing beads. Cut beads, adding ³⁄₁₆″ seam allowance.

3. Trace the motif pattern pieces from the back of the book onto the proper butcher paper shape with black ink. Place fabric of chosen color on

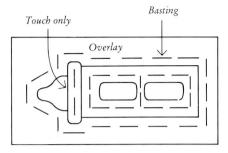

DIAGRAM 1

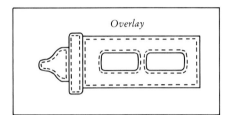

DIAGRAM 2

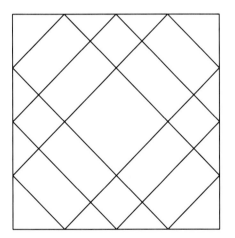

DIAGRAM 3

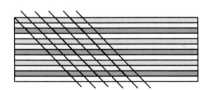

DIAGRAM 4

pattern and trace using a no. 2½ lead pencil. Trace all motifs of same color fabric onto fabric at one time. Join the fabric to lightweight fusible interfacing following manufacturer's instructions so it will adhere properly.

4. Cut out all motif shapes just inside the drawn pencil line. You do not want any lines to show through the voile overlay. NOTE: Do not add seam allowance. Set aside the cut motifs; handle each one as little as possible so the edges do not fray.

5. Begin with the baby bottle in the rectangle. Place the white ground rectangle on butcher paper pattern for placement of fabric motif pieces and use a small dab of fabric glue stick under all the fabric motifs so they will stay put on the ground fabric as you appliqué. NOTE: Since colors may show through one another, motifs must just touch one another.

6. Place voile overlay over prepared ground square. Baste with large stitches around the entire design. *(See diagram 1.)*

7. Choose thread the color of the motif. Appliqué, using the running stitch. Stitch through all three layers of fabric, barely inside the cut edge of the motif. *(See diagram 2.)*

8. Continue in this manner until all rectangles have been appliquéd. Then do the small squares and finally the center square. NOTE: Add letters to baby bracelet with running stitch.

9. Press the blocks. See instructions in Finishing page 128.

10. Set the quilt together. Use diagram 3 as a guide. Press all seams open.

11. Appliqué sashing beads over the seam lines using the tack or ladder stitch turning under ³⁄₁₆″ seam allowance. NOTE: You may find it easier to appliqué the sashing beads on as you stitch each block to its neighbor. The work will be less bulky to handle.

12. Add mitred border. See Borders, Mitred page 133. Press all seams open. Use scalloped border guide to draw scalloped edge. See patterns in the back of the book.

13. Appliqué sashing beads over the seam lines around the seam where the quilt top and border are joined.

14. Make binding fabric by sewing alternating strips of each color into a rectangle. Press seams open. Cut bias binding 2″ wide by folding along diagonal of rectangle. Piece bias strips to make 9 yds. of binding. See Bias Preparation page 23. *(See diagram 4.)*

To finish the quilt see Finishing, chapter 13, for instructions on pressing the completed quilt top, preparing batting, preparing backing, assembling three layers, and quilting (quilt just outside motif edges; use photograph as a guide). Now scallop the borders following the instructions on page 134 and add the binding you prepared in step 14.

Chapter 9

~

REVERSE APPLIQUÉ

REVERSE APPLIQUÉ IS SOMETIMES FOUND ON NINETEENTH-CENTURY QUILTS, molas from the San Blas Islands, Hmong Pa ndau, and some Hawaiian quilts. The beauty of appliqué is exemplified in this technique.

Just as the name implies, the technique is the opposite of basic appliqué. The top fabric is removed to reveal the ground fabric or several other fabrics layered underneath.

The first time appliquérs hear the term *reverse appliqué* a sense of fear and foreboding comes upon them. The feeling continues until they try the dreaded technique and then...they can't be stopped. Reverse appliqué is *not* difficult. Once you get the hang of it, it is easy and extremely rewarding. Corners are square, points are sharp, and circles are round. Just follow the reverse appliqué instructions found in Essentials page 25.

Hearts and Trees Quilt, *courtesy of The Ardis & Robert James Collection*

HEARTS AND TREES QUILT

Navy blue with tiny white pin dots is, for me, the perfect fabric for this spectacular quilt or any quilt. I love intricate designs—hearts, tiny circles, and birds. This design was the quiltmaker's original. She even included her initials in one corner. Wee squares and rectangles are appliquéd to form the letters B and J. This piece is also beautifully quilted with cross-hatching, double-stitched pumpkin seeds, and outlining—all done with tiny, exquisite stitches.

Reverse appliqué hearts in the leaf design are appliquéd over the junction of the blocks. The birds' eyes, the tiny crosses in the stars, and the handles of the tiny vases in the border are also reverse appliquéd. The grapes are perfect tiny circles. Many of the motifs have two or more pieces to a leaf, a vine, a stem, or a basket handle, as if the maker did not have enough fabric.

Our anonymous quiltmaker was a master!

HEARTS AND TREES QUILT

STITCHING TECHNIQUES	Tack, ladder
SETTING	Straight set
FABRIC SUGGESTIONS	
Ground	White solid
Motifs	Navy blue and white pin dot
Backing	White solid
Binding	Same navy blue pin dot

	TWIN	DOUBLE/QUEEN	KING
FINISHED SIZE	66″ × 96″	81″ × 96″	96″ × 111″
BLOCKS SET	3 × 5	4 × 5	5 × 6
15″ × 15″ BLOCKS	15	20	30

YARDAGE

	TWIN	DOUBLE/QUEEN	KING
GROUND: **Blocks and borders**	6½	7½	10
MOTIFS	6¾	8	10½
BACKING	6	6	9¾
BATTING	70″ × 100″	85″ × 100″	100″ × 115″
BINDING	½	⅝	¾

CUTTING

	TWIN	DOUBLE/QUEEN	KING
BLOCKS 17″ × 17″	15	20	30
MOTIFS			
Large trees	15	20	30
Tubs	15	20	30
Birds	4	4	4
Tiny vases	4	4	4
4-heart leaves	8	12	20
3-heart leaves	8	10	12
2-heart leaves	4	4	4
Leaves and grapes	25	29	35
Large leaves	8	8	8
Stars	12	12	12
Vines, bias tube	1″	1″	1″
Vines, bias tube	1½″	1½″	1½″
BORDER WIDTH	11″	11″	11″
BACKING LENGTHS	2	2	3
BINDING WIDTH	1½″	1½″	1½″

CONSTRUCTION

1. Prepare a large block pattern. See Pattern Preparation page 20.

2. Prepare templates. See About Templates page 20. See also patterns at the end of the book.

3. Prepare fabric motif shapes using one of the methods detailed in Essentials.

4. Prepare bias tubes according to instructions in Bias Preparation page 23.

5. Center a block of ground fabric right side up on the pattern, and pin the fabric motif shapes in place.

6. Starting on the bottom of the tub, *not* at a corner, use your round wooden toothpick to turn under ³⁄₁₆″ seam allowance. Appliqué using tack or ladder stitch.

7. Continue the appliqué on the outside edge of the tree. Reverse appliqué the heart. NOTE: Set your work down often on a flat surface and smooth it to prevent puckering.

8. Trim block to 15½″ × 15½″, centering design. Press block following instructions in Finishing page 128.

9. Continue in this manner, following steps 5–8 until all blocks are complete.

10. Stitch all rows together, following photograph for orientation. See Straight Set page 128.

11. Press seams open.

12. Center 4-heart leaves between blocks using photograph as a guide, and appliqué in place. NOTE: Reverse appliqué the heart in the center of each leaf. See Reverse Appliqué page 25.

13. Prepare border pattern by cutting two 11″×36″ strips of butcher paper. Tape them together to form a corner. Copy the design onto the paper.

14. Cut border fabric. See Borders, Squared page 132. Place ground fabric border strip right side up on pattern and mark with pencil a broken line down the center of the vine for placement of bias strip. See Border Patterns page 20. NOTE: Move pattern as needed to finish entire border strip.

15. Stitch border strips onto quilt top. See Borders page 132.

16. Continue the appliqué:

    a. The 3-heart leaves around outside edge of quilt center.

    b. The 2-heart leaves around outside edge of quilt center.

    c. The birds in corners of quilt center. NOTE: Reverse appliqué eyes.

17. Using the large border pattern as a guide, pin grapes, leaves, stars, and tiny vase in place.

18. Appliqué tiny vase and stars in place. NOTE: Reverse appliqué handles in vase and crosses in centers of stars.

19. Continue the appliqué starting in the center of the side border strip. Pin bias tube following drawn line; appliqué in place. NOTE: Tuck under stems.

20. You may appliqué the entire vine, then the leaves, grapes, and stems or you may appliqué parts of each as you go—a little vine, a stem, a leaf, grapes, and so on.

To finish the quilt, see Finishing, chapter 13, for instructions on pressing the completed quilt top, preparing the batting, preparing the backing, assembling three layers, quilting, and binding.

Mola Quilt, *appliquéd by Jeri Fountain and quilted by Laurene Sinema*

MOLA QUILT

Many of the Cuna Indian women of the San Blas Islands (off Panama's east coast) are needle artists of the highest degree. They design and appliqué colorful intricate folk art panels that are stitched into blouses. *Mola* is the Cuna word for either the blouse or the separate panel. The authentic molas have become collectors' items and can be purchased in various cultural gift shops across the nation.

Perhaps you own one or more. Are they resting in a drawer or on the shelf of a cupboard waiting to be matted and framed, or stitched into a pillow, or used to decorate a skirt or blouse? I have several. We used one of them in the wall quilt pictured here. The two birds gaze thoughtfully at each other for the center mola.

I have an exciting plan for you and your mola. If you do not own one, you must find the perfect one. Or, use the pattern here to copy my traditional mola. This wall quilt consists of a design for a border that will frame any large mola. The border has four small corner molas, and the border can be adjusted to fit any size center.

The whimsical birds, turtle, and fish were a delight to design. Since my mola has a black overlay, the four corners and the border also have black overlays. The second-layer fabrics pick up all the colors in the center mola: hot pink, red, blue, yellow, green, and white. The designs appear difficult, but the technique is simple.

The backing fabric is a Hoffman geometric design with a black ground that holds all the bright colors in the molas. It gives the piece yet another dimension.

Jeri Fountain, an avid appliquér, agreed to put into fabric this plan of mine. She loves working with black. Jeri's appliqué is flawless as evidenced in the *Mola Quilt.* Isn't it splendid?

If you choose your own mola, your mola wall quilt becomes one of a kind. But you can also make other innovations to have a unique piece. Perhaps your overlay fabric will be red or orange. Be sure to look for an unusual but compatible print for the backing fabric.

MOLA QUILT

STITCHING TECHNIQUES	Tack, ladder
SETTING	Center block with borders and corner blocks
FABRIC SUGGESTIONS	*All solids*
Center block	black, white, and various bright solids
Border	To match your center mola overlay
Various layer fabrics	To match all other fabrics in center mola
Backing	Print to coordinate
Binding	Same as overlay fabric
FINISHED SIZE	Sample is 23″ × 27″

YARDAGE

CENTER BLOCK	
Overlay	½
Ground	½
Various layer fabrics	⅛ each
BORDER	
Overlay	1
Various layer fabrics	¼ most predominate
	⅙ all others
BACKING	1
BINDING	¼
EMBROIDERY FLOSS	Various colors

CUTTING

CENTER MOLA IN SAMPLE	
Overlay 13″ × 17″	1
Ground 13″ × 17″	1
SHORT BORDER OVERLAY 6½″ × 13″	2
LONG BORDER OVERLAY 6½″ × 17″	2
CORNER SQUARES OVERLAY 6½″ × 6½″	4
VARIOUS COLORED FABRICS	Cut each underlay as you are ready to appliqué
BACKING	Sample is 25″ × 29″
BINDING WIDTH	1½″

1. Prepare a master pattern to plan placement of various color fabrics. Or you may wish to plan as you go. Use patterns in the back of the book.

2. Use light box or daylight window to trace entire pattern onto overlay fabric. Mark areas to be reverse appliquéd.

3. Start appliqué on shortest border. Measure first area to be appliquéd. Cut square or rectangle of colored fabric to be placed under the overlay.

4. With sharp pointed scissors, make snips in the overlay in each of the areas to be appliquéd. The rectangle will be cut down the center with one half the seam allowance to be appliquéd under each side. Make sure your snip is straight and true. *(See diagram 1.)*

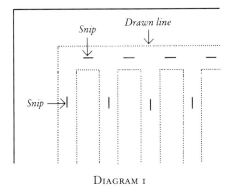

DIAGRAM 1

5. Place underlay fabric beneath overlay as necessary and baste the entire design through all layers. *(See diagram 2.)* REMEMBER: This is reverse appliqué. Do *not* baste where the snips have been taken. See Reverse Appliqué page 25.

6. Cut the first rectangle down the center to ¼″ from each end. Clip diagonally into the corner on both sides. *(See diagram 3.)*

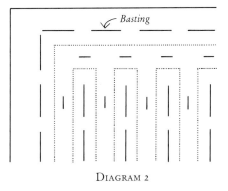

DIAGRAM 2

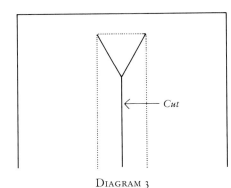

DIAGRAM 3

7. Using a round wooden toothpick, turn under seam allowance and finger press. Start the appliqué in the center of the rectangle using the tack stitch, and continue around the rectangle.

8. Set work down on a flat surface often and smooth it to prevent puckering. Continue in this manner until all border strips are completed.

9. Center mola and corner molas are basted and appliquéd as above. *Watch for:*
   - Eyes: Pupils are appliquéd on top after white is reverse appliquéd.
   - Fish teeth: Teeth are 3-dimensional, made of tiny squares folded into triangles and appliquéd into place.
   - Running stitch: Embroider as on pattern.
   - Center mola, bird body: Second color fabric is appliquéd on top of first color. Stitch as shown on pattern.

10. Press, following instructions in Finishing page 128.

11. Trim border strips to 6″ × 12½″ and 6″ × 16½″.

12. Trim corner molas to 6″ × 6″ squares.

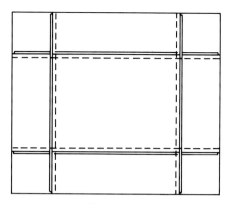

DIAGRAM 4

13. Trim center mola to 12½″ × 16½″.

14. Stitch borders to center mola, using ¼″ seam allowance. Press seams into borders. *(See diagram 4.)*

15. Center the quilt top on backing fabric with wrong sides together. NOTE: No batting is used in this quilt.

16. Quilt ¼″ outside the center mola seam line.

17. Add binding; see page 136.

If, as you finish, you are completely hooked on this appliqué style, you will find Charlotte Patera's book *Mola Making*, or *Molas* by Rhoda L. Auld, invaluable. They are full of history, technique, and designs.

Pa ndau Table Runner/Wall Quilt

"What is Pa ndau?" I can hear you asking the question. Perhaps you have not heard the term *Pa ndau,* but you may have heard of the Hmong. They are mountain people who emigrated from China in the midnineteenth century and settled in what is now Laos, Cambodia, and North Vietnam. During the war in Vietnam many Hmong men risked their lives to help the Americans. They and their families were ultimately driven out of their homes to Thailand, and from Thailand they came to the United States. They came with few belongings and a desire for freedom for their families.

The Hmong women whom I have met have all been eager to show their beautiful needlework, Pa ndau. I, in turn, have been eager to see the Pa ndau and to see the women actually do the stitching. I met one beautiful young girl dressed in her native costume. The skirt was elaborately appliquéd in the geometric reverse appliqué of the Pa ndau. It was absolutely breathtaking especially when paired with her blouse and headdress.

Perhaps you have seen Pa ndau summer coverlets. Shades of blue or beige with blue are popular color combinations. The Hmong women also make pillow covers, pincushions, and even tiny hearts on strings to be worn as necklaces.

The black and red wall quilt or table runner included here will take some time. You may wish to do only one of the panels and finish it into a pillow. The five quilt blocks are authentic Pa ndau that originally were pillow covers. My friend Janet Carruth owned them and offered them when I began searching for something unusual for you. She agreed to have them set together into this wall quilt or table runner and and is pleased by the final quilt.

Authentic Pa ndau,
set together by Janet Carruth

PA NDAU TABLE RUNNER/WALL QUILT

STITCHING TECHNIQUE	Tack
SETTING	Straight set
FABRIC SUGGESTIONS	*All solids*
Ground	Red or black
Overlay	With red ground use black
	With black ground use red
Backing	Print to coordinate
Binding	Red or black
FINISHED SIZE	16″ × 80″
16″ × 16″ BLOCKS	5

YARDAGE

GROUND, OVERLAY, AND BINDING	1½ each color
BACKING	1½

CUTTING

GROUND AND OVERLAY 18″ × 18″	5 each
BACKING	20″ × 84″ pieced to size
BINDING WIDTH	1½″

CONSTRUCTION

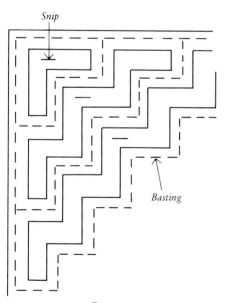

Snip

Basting

DIAGRAM 5

1. Prepare a master pattern. See Pattern Preparation page 20.

2. Trace entire design on your overlay fabric using a light box or a daylight window using a light-colored pencil. Mark the areas to be reverse appliquéd.

3. With sharp pointed scissors make a snip in the center of each row that will be cut away to reveal ground fabric. NOTE: Half the row will be appliquéd on each side, so your snip must be straight and true.

4. Place marked and snipped overlay fabric right side up on right side of ground fabric. Pin in place.

5. Baste the entire block. Using tiny basting stitches, baste down center of every row that has not been snipped. Break threads when an area is completed. Baste around entire outside edge of block. *(See diagram 5.)* Set work down often on flat surface and smooth it with your hands to keep it from puckering.

6. Start appliqué on a center rickrack design. Place tiny sharp pointed scissors into your original snip and cut down the center of the row, to within ⅛″ of the end. Cut diagonally into corners to the drawn line. *(See diagram 6.)*

7. Using a round wooden toothpick, turn under seam allowance. Finger press. NOTE: I place the work on a flat surface to start. It is easier to use the toothpick and finger press when you have both hands free.

8. With seam allowance turned under, appliqué using the tack stitch. Be sure to stitch both sides of the cut area.

9. Continue in this manner until all center rickrack designs have been appliquéd. NOTE: To keep the rows even and straight, you must take tiny stitches.

10. Start cutting the spiral elephant's foot design at the outside point. Work toward the center, cutting only an inch at a time. *(See diagram 7.)*

11. Using a round wooden toothpick turn under seam allowance. Finger press and appliqué using the tack stitch. Appliqué both sides of spiral as you work to the center.

12. Continue to cut and appliqué until the entire block is completed.

13. The outside edge of overlay will be cut away when final row is appliquéd, leaving a border of the ground fabric.

14. Press following instructions in Finishing page 128.

15. Continue in this manner, following steps 2–14. NOTE: You will have 3 blocks of one design and 2 blocks of the other design—3 with black overlay, 2 with red overlay.

16. Trim blocks to 16½″ × 16½″ and stitch together in one row, alternating designs.

17. Press seam allowances open.

18. Center your top on backing fabric, wrong sides together with no batting.

19. Hand quilt ¼″ on either side of seams.

20. Add binding. See Binding page 136.

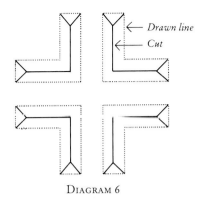

Drawn line
Cut

DIAGRAM 6

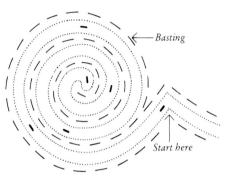

Basting

Start here

DIAGRAM 7

Chapter 10

~

NINETEENTH-CENTURY FOLK ART QUILTS

In *Folk Painters of America,* Robert Bishop describes folk art in the early and midnineteenth century as "fresh, imaginative, simple, and primitive." This art form comes from the areas outside the more sophisticated cities—the farms and rural villages. The artist, whether a wood-carver or a quiltmaker, used the animals, trees, houses, barns, and family members as models. Patriotism ran high in this era and is reflected in much of the art. Many of the album quilts of the 1840–1860 period include eagles and flags in the blocks.

My interest in folk art began years ago. I love the primitive shapes and the bright colors used by the artists. When I began teaching and researching the Baltimore Album quilts it became obvious that album quilts made during the same time period (1840–1860) but not in the immediate Baltimore area did not have the same refinement of design. The quilts made in outlying areas of Pennsylvania, New York, and New Jersey had what I term folk art interpretations of the Baltimore Album designs. They are simple and naive. They capture your sense of beauty and tickle your funny bone.

Two quilts are included in this section: a glorious antique quilt and a charming wall quilt. *Flowers and Grapes in Sawtooth Wheel* is an antique quilt with a bold design full of red and purple grapes. Leaves, vines, blossoms, and a funky sort of bud or leaf also cover the quilt. The wall quilt features nine miniature pineapple designs from antique quilts that form the center of this delightful hanging.

Either of these quilts will be a challenge for you. Choose your fabrics and get started immediately on the quilt that appeals the most. Good luck!

Flowers and Grapes in Sawtooth Wheel Quilt, *courtesy of The Ardis & Robert James Collection*

Flowers and Grapes in Sawtooth Wheel Quilt

A tiny print on white forms the ground for the robust design of this Mennonite quilt made in Pennsylvania. Red, green, purple, and orange solids are used in the vines, grapes, leaves, flowers, and sawtooth motifs. Every smidgen of space is filled with color and dramatic design, making this an exciting quilt for a bed or to hang on a wall.

As you appliqué the large blocks you must carefully watch the placement of all the motifs because circles can so easily become ovals. The floral, sawtooth, large and small leaf, and vine motifs will be easy to appliqué. The challenge will be the many, many circles. When you finish this quilt you will be a master at circles!

The hand quilting is unusual on this quilt because the red motifs were quilted inside in red thread, the green motifs inside in green thread, and the orange motifs and the ground were done in white thread. Typically all the quilting of this era was in white thread. The outline quilting outside the appliqué motifs is ⅛″ from the edge. The narrow green inner border is magnificently quilted.

FLOWERS AND GRAPES IN SAWTOOTH WHEEL QUILT

STITCHING TECHNIQUES	Tack, blind
SETTING	Straight set
FABRIC SUGGESTIONS	
Ground	
Blocks and borders	Small white print
Motifs	
Grapes	Purple and red solids
Vines and leaves	Green and black solids
Triangles	Red solid
Flowers	Red, green, and pumpkin solids
Inner and outer rings	Green solid
Inner border	Black solid
Backing	White solid
Binding	Red solid

	DOUBLE/QUEEN	KING
FINISHED SIZE	84″ × 84″	116″ × 116″
BLOCKS SET	2 × 2	3 × 3
32″ × 32″ BLOCKS	4	9

YARDAGE

	DOUBLE/QUEEN	KING
GROUND		
Blocks and borders	6¾	12
MOTIFS		
Red—grapes, triangles, flowers, binding	3½	4½
Purple—grapes	¾	1
Green—vine, leaves, inner and outer rings, and flowers	3	4½
Pumpkin—flower centers	⅛	⅛
Black—inner border and outer bias vines	1½	2
BACKING	5	10
BATTING	88″ × 88″	120″ × 120″

CUTTING

	DOUBLE/QUEEN	KING
GROUND		
Blocks 34″ × 34″	4	9
MOTIFS		
Red		
Grapes	288	376
Triangle ring	4	9
Flower circle	5	13
Half circle	4	8
Quarter circle	4	4
Purple		
Grapes	304	400
Green		
Oval leaves	128	288
Medium leaves	44	72
Large leaves	32	72
Center flowers	5	13
Half flowers	4	8
Quarter flowers	4	4
Bias tube (1½″)	26 yds.	42 yds.
Pumpkin		
Flower centers	5	13
Black		
Bias tube (1½″)	16 yds.	36 yds.
INNER BORDER WIDTH	2½″	2½″
OUTER BORDER WIDTH	8½″	8½″
BACKING LENGTHS	2	3
BINDING WIDTH	1½″	1½″

1. Prepare a large block pattern. See Pattern Preparation page 20.

2. Prepare templates. See About Templates page 20. See Template Patterns in the back of the book.

3. Prepare fabric motif shapes using one of the methods detailed in Essentials.

4. Prepare bias tube according to instructions in Bias Preparation page 23. The strips are cut 1½″ wide and are sewn to ½″ wide.

5. Center a block of ground fabric right side up on pattern and pin center flower fabric shapes in place.

6. Using a round wooden toothpick, turn under seam allowance on center circle shape, and appliqué the circle using tack or ladder stitch, clipping curves as necessary. See Circles page 32. NOTE: Take tiny stitches as you appliqué so the curves are round and smooth.

7. Continue by appliquéing:
   - Four inner petal shapes, keeping the distance between each petal an even ¼″.
   - Outer petal piece.

8. Center the block on the pattern and mark with pencil a broken line down the center of the inner ring, the outer ring, and the grape and leaf stems. Pin inner oval-shaped leaves and triangles in place.

9. Continue by appliquéing:
   - Inner oval-shaped leaves; leave raw edges flat under bias ring.
   - Triangles; leave raw edges flat under bias ring.
   - Outer curve of inner bias ring over triangles, centered over broken line.

- Inner curve of inner bias ring over oval-shaped leaves. Turn under bias end and appliqué in place.
- Outer oval-shaped leaves; leave raw edges flat under bias ring.
- Stems centered over marked broken line; leave raw edges flat under bias ring.
- Outer curve of outer bias ring over triangles, centered over marked broken line.
- Inner curve of outer bias ring over oval-shaped leaves. Turn under bias end and appliqué in place.

10. Center block on pattern and mark with pencil a dot in center of each grape.

11. Continue by appliquéing:
- All leaves in place.
- All grapes on marked dots. See Circles page 32 for information on making grapes.

12. Trim block to 32½″ × 32½″, centering design. Press block following instructions in Finishing page 128.

13. Continue in this manner following steps 5–12 until all blocks are completed.

14. Stitch the blocks together following instructions in Straight Set page 128. Press seams open.

15. Pin fabric flower shapes in place centered over the intersecting seams, halves on edges, and quarters on corners. *(See diagram 1.)*

16. Appliqué following steps 6 and 7.

17. Prepare outer border pattern by cutting two 8″ × 36″ strips of butcher paper. Tape them together to form a corner and copy the design onto the paper.

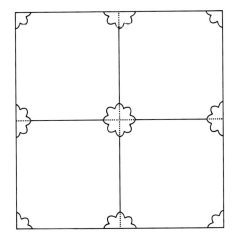

DIAGRAM I

18. Cut border fabric; see Borders, Squared page 132. Place ground fabric border strip right side up on pattern and mark with pencil a broken line down the center of the vine for placement of bias strip. Mark center of grape stems and leaves. Mark a dot in the center of each grape. Move pattern as needed to finish entire border strip. See Border Patterns page 20.

19. Pin leaves in place. Pin bias tube following the drawn line. NOTE: Tuck under leaves and grape stems as you did on the blocks.

20. You may appliqué the vine, then the leaves and grapes, or you may appliqué some of each as you go—a little vine, grapes and a leaf, and so on. NOTE: Appliqué to within 18″ of the corners on all border strips.

21. Press borders following instructions in Finishing page 128.

22. Stitch inner border strips to quilt top. See Borders, Squared page 132.

23. Stitch outer borders to quilt top as you did inner borders. When all borders are attached, complete the appliqué.

To finish the quilt, see Finishing, chapter 13, for instructions on pressing the completed quilt top, preparing the batting, preparing the backing, assembling three layers, quilting, and binding.

Pineapple Miniature Quilt, *appliquéd and quilted by Betty Alderman*

PINEAPPLE MINIATURE QUILT

In the past three years I have been drafting designs from antique album quilts made during the 1840–1860 era. I have also started to scale down some of these designs to miniature sizes. The blocks that are the most appealing to me are the folk art or the more primitive and naive patterns.

For this quilt I chose to take pineapple designs from antique quilts, using only one-fourth of the block, downsize them to four inches, and turn them on point. My friend Betty Alderman of Mansfield, Ohio, came to visit at the time the idea struck. Betty, who is extremely creative, is also a quilter, a painter, and a designer. She took the idea home to Ohio and located the designs for the pineapples and the bird on the branch. She put it all into fabric and hand appliquéd and hand quilted this delightful miniature quilt.

Reverse appliqué and stitchery enhance the designs. The hand quilting is exquisite with clam shells in a portion of the border, cross-hatching in the corner triangles, and stippling in some of the blocks.

This charming wall quilt will be an heirloom to be admired and inherited by many generations of your family. It will be a tribute to your fine handiwork!

PINEAPPLE MINIATURE QUILT

STITCHING TECHNIQUES	Tack, ladder, buttonhole, outline
SETTING	On point
FABRIC SUGGESTIONS	
Ground	Off-white solid
Sashing, binding, and border	Turkey red solid
Motifs	Red prints and solids, green prints and solids, gold prints and solids
Backing	Off-white solid
FINISHED SIZE	27″ × 27″
BLOCKS SET	3 × 3
4″ × 4″ BLOCKS	9

YARDAGE

GROUND, BORDER, BACKING	1⅔
MOTIFS	
Border leaves, birds, and pineapples leaves	½
Pineapples	6″ × 6″ squares of a variety of fabrics
SASHING, BINDING, AND PARTS OF MOTIFS	1
BATTING	31″ × 31″
EMBROIDERY FLOSS	Various colors

CUTTING

GROUND	
Blocks 6″ × 6″	9
Corner triangles 11″ × 11″ × 15½″	4
MOTIFS	
Birds (bodies and wings)	2 red bodies, 2 red wings
	2 green bodies, 2 green wings
	4 gold wings
Border pineapples	4 red
Border pineapple leaves	
Large	4 green
Small	16 green
Branches and buds	4 green, 4 red
Pineapples, all individual	9 various colors *(see photo)*
SASHING WIDTH	1″
INNER BORDER WIDTH	1″
OUTER BORDER WIDTH	3½″
BACKING LENGTH	1
BINDING WIDTH	1½″

CONSTRUCTION

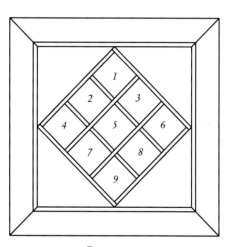

DIAGRAM 2

1. Prepare the block and corner triangle patterns. See Pattern Preparation page 20. See Template Patterns in the back of the book.

2. Prepare templates. See About Templates page 20.

3. Prepare fabric motif shapes using one of the methods detailed in Essentials, adding a ³⁄₁₆″ seam allowance. NOTE: Make a tiny snip for reverse appliqué in patterns no. 1 and no. 5 and the four border pineapples. See Reverse Appliqué page 25 for instructions.

4. Center a block of ground fabric right side up on pineapple no. 1 pattern *(see diagram 2)* and pin the motif shapes in place on the ground fabric. NOTE: Insert fabric under the pineapple for reverse appliqué.

5. Using a round wooden toothpick, turn under ³⁄₁₆″ seam allowance, and start the appliqué on an outer curve of the pineapple using either tack or ladder stitch. NOTE: As you reach the inner curves, you must clip to the drawn line as described in Stitches page 32.

6. To reverse appliqué the center, see Reverse Appliqué page 25. NOTE: Set your work down often on a flat surface and smooth it to keep it from puckering.

7. Appliqué the green top of the pineapple.

8. Trim block to 4½″ × 4½″. Press the block following instructions in Finishing page 128.

9. Continue in this manner, appliquéing all the blocks following steps 4–8. *Some hints:*

- Block no. 2—Appliqué 2 side leaves, top leaf, and finally pineapple over raw edges of the leaves.
- Block no. 3—Appliqué large leaves first, overlapping them leaving the overlapped and bottom edges flat. Appliqué the smaller leaves. Appliqué the pineapple last, covering the bottom raw edges of leaves.
- Block no. 4—Appliqué 2 side gold leaves first. Then appliqué the pineapple on top covering inner raw edges of leaves. Appliqué the diamond at the bottom and small leaves on top and bottom. NOTE: Betty added a decorative green buttonhole stitch around the leaves because the gold fabric seemed too pale. Good idea!
- Block no. 5—Appliqué the pineapple after inserting the inlay fabric beneath the pineapple. Tuck in top leaves and pin them for later work as you appliqué the pineapple. Appliqué the bottom leaf over the raw edge of the pineapple. Finally, appliqué the four top leaves.
- Block no. 6—Appliqué outside gold leaves first leaving entire inner edge raw under oval pineapple. Appliqué pineapple. Add gold teardrops on top of the pineapple. Appliqué 2 green teardrops on each side and 3 leaves on very top.
- Block no. 7—Tuck pineapple inside leaves. Appliqué leaves in place, folding in seam allowance of pineapple at top. Appliqué pineapple top, then appliqué the 2 side leaves.
- Block no. 8—Appliqué pineapple first and then leaves around sides and bottom. The raw edge of the pineapple is flat at the very bottom. The leaves are appliquéd over it.
- Block no. 9—Appliqué the green outer points first. Appliqué the 3 gold strips across the center. Appliqué the red circle, covering the raw edges of points and strips. Appliqué the top leaves and bottom triangle last.

10. Sew blocks and sashings together. See Straight Set with Sashing page 129.

11. Cut and attach first inner border. See Borders, Squared page 132.

12. Center triangle fabric right side up on pattern for placement of bird, branch, leaf, and bud motifs. Pin them in place.

13. Appliqué branch, buds and leaves. Appliqué the red body of bird and then the wings, gold first.

14. Press the triangle following instructions in Finishing page 128.

15. Complete all triangles following steps 12–14. Attach triangles to quilt top center.

16. Cut narrow and wide outside border strips; see Borders, Mitred page 133.

17. Center the wide border strip right side up on pattern, and pin all leaf motifs in place using the photo as a guide. Starting on an outer curve, turn under seam allowance on largest leaf and appliqué in place. Appliqué smaller leaf motifs.

18. Press border strip following instructions in Finishing page 128.

19. Continue in this manner following steps 17 and 18 until all borders are complete. NOTE: Corner motifs will not be appliquéd until after the border corners are mitred.

20. Sew narrow and wide outside borders together. Attach borders to quilt top. See Borders, Mitred page 133.

21. Pin pineapple motifs in place on mitred border corners. Appliqué.

To finish the quilt, see Finishing, chapter 13, for instructions on pressing the completed quilt top, preparing the batting, preparing the backing, assembling three layers, quilting, and binding.

STIPPLE QUILTING

Chapter 11

∽

NINETEENTH-CENTURY TRADITIONAL APPLIQUÉ

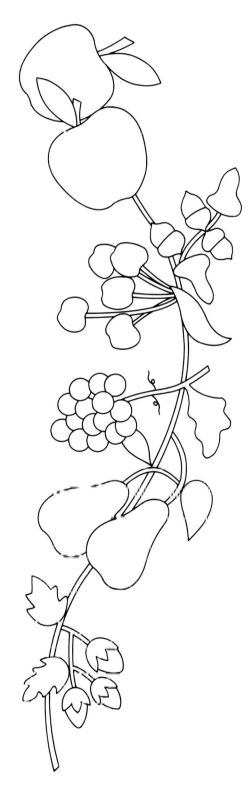

DURING THE NINETEENTH CENTURY, QUILTS AND QUILTING ABOUNDED. Quilts were made for many occasions—a Presentation quilt honoring a community leader; an Album quilt for a bride-to-be; a Freedom quilt for a young man reaching legal age. A group of friends often made the quilt blocks, stitched them together, and then got together at a quilting bee to do the quilting. The bee was a social gathering. The women quilted all day, and in the evening, the men arrived for dinner and dancing.

Quilts were made to be used. Often the entire family participated in the making of a quilt. Children threaded needles; husbands and fiancés suggested and drew patterns; wives and grandmothers stitched. They needed many quilts, and their quiltmaking endeavors continued over months and years, enjoyed by all.

The midnineteenth-century appliqué quilts are my favorites. I delight in the colors, the fabrics, the designs, and the glorious hand quilting. Many of them are red and green on white grounds with touches of gold. Some have large blocks, sometimes only four in a quilt top, covered with large floral motifs. Other quilt blocks are smaller with intricate floral designs. The pictorial quilt blocks depict memorials, birds, people, buildings, flags, ships. Each of the depictions says something about the recipient of the quilt.

This chapter includes a taste of nineteenth-century quilts. The small blocks of the *Mexican Rose Quilt* are a surprise because at first glance the large diamond-shaped leaves appear to be the connecting units. The dog's tooth inner border is a perfect divider between the busy, busy top and the gentle, quiet outer border.

A design taken from an antique Baltimore Album quilt forms the center of the other quilt in the chapter. Both of these quilts will test your appliqué know-how and proficiency. The hours spent on either will be therapy to your soul and increase your expertise. Do consider making both of them.

Mexican Rose Quilt, *courtesy of The Ardis & Robert James Collection*

Mexican Rose Quilt

The block on this quilt is difficult to locate. When you realize it is set on point, you easily see both the primary and secondary designs. The quilt top is totally appliquéd, almost every square inch. Each full block, half block, and quarter block has a portion of the design. The fabrics are a solid red with yellow and teal calicos on a solid white ground. The addition of the dog's tooth border gives a nice break between the blocks and the outer border.

The blocks are hand quilted in diagonal lines one-half inch apart. Straight feathers are quilted on both sides of the stem. On the border, leaves the same shape as the appliquéd leaves have been quilted along the vine.

This quilt will take many hours to appliqué only because it is so filled with appliqué—not because it is difficult. The teardrop petals, leaves, and round center motifs are all large and easy to stitch.

MEXICAN ROSE QUILT

STITCHING TECHNIQUES	Tack, ladder
SETTING	Diagonal set
FABRIC SUGGESTIONS	
Ground	Off-white solid
Motifs	
Flowers and centers	Red solid, yellow solid
Leaves and dog's tooth border	Teal print
Backing	Off-white solid
Binding	Off-white solid

	TWIN	DOUBLE/QUEEN	KING
FINISHED SIZE	75″×94″	94″×94″	113″×113″
BLOCKS SET	3×4	4×4	5×5
13½″ × 13½″ BLOCKS	18	25	41

YARDAGE

	TWIN	DOUBLE/QUEEN	KING
GROUND			
Blocks, borders, binding	6¾	8¼	11¾
MOTIFS			
Red: flower petals and centers	2¾	3½	5¼
Yellow: flower petals and centers	¾	1	1¼
Teal: large and small leaves, bias vine and stems, dog's tooth	5	5¾	7¾
BACKING	5½	8¼	9¾
BATTING	79″×98″	98″×98″	117″×117″

CUTTING

	TWIN	DOUBLE/QUEEN	KING
GROUND			
Blocks 15½″ × 15½″	18	25	41
Side triangles 14½″ × 14½″ × 20½″	10	12	16
Corner triangles 11″ × 11″ × 15½″	4	4	4
MOTIFS			
Red flower petals	576	768	1200
Red centers, small	20	24	32
Yellow flower petals	40	48	64
Yellow centers, large	32	41	61
small	92	124	196
Teal leaves, large	96	128	200
small	60	72	96
Dog's tooth strip	to fit border	to fit border	to fit border
Vine and stems, bias tube (1″)	30 yds.	38 yds.	58 yds.
INNER DOG'S TOOTH BORDER WIDTH	2¼″	2¼″	2¼″
OUTER BORDER WIDTH	8″	8″	8″
BACKING LENGTHS	2	3	3
BINDING WIDTH	1½″	1½″	1½″

CONSTRUCTION

1. Prepare a large block pattern. See Pattern Preparation page 20. See patterns at the end of the book for the full blocks and for the side and corner triangles.

2. Prepare templates. See About Templates page 20.

3. Prepare fabric shapes using one of the methods detailed in Essentials. NOTE: Add ³⁄₁₆″ seam allowance.

4. Prepare bias tube. See Bias Preparation page 23. The strips are cut 1″ wide and sewn to ¼″ wide.

5. Center block of ground fabric right side up on the pattern. Pin fabric motif shapes in place on the ground fabric. NOTE: Place flower petals, stems, and leaves under large and small circles.

6. Using round wooden toothpick, turn under ³⁄₁₆″ seam allowance. Start the appliqué on the large leaf just under the yellow center using the tack or ladder stitch. NOTE: The raw edge of the leaf under the yellow center will be left flat.

7. Continue the appliqué, first finishing all large leaves and then all bias stems. Finally, using the toothpick to turn under a ³⁄₁₆″ seam allowance, appliqué all large yellow centers. Leave the raw ends of bias flat under the yellow centers. Then appliqué all flower petals, making sure they are evenly spaced. The bottom raw edge of each petal will be flat under the yellow center. Finally, appliqué the small yellow centers.

8. Trim block to 14″ × 14.″ Press block following instructions in Finishing page 128.

9. Continue in this manner following steps 5–8 until all blocks and side and corner triangles are completed.

10. Stitch blocks together. See Diagonal Set page 130.

11. Make dog's tooth border. Cut inner border fabric, see Borders, Squared page 132 for length. Attach dog's tooth strip right side up on right side of fabric aligning raw edges. See Sawtooth or Dog's Tooth page 134.

12. Attach the top and bottom dog's tooth strip borders to quilt top. Then attach the sides and appliqué small squares to the corners.

13. Prepare border pattern by cutting two 9″ × 36″ strips of butcher paper. Tape them together to form a corner, and copy the design from patterns in the back of the book onto the paper. Cut outer borders; see Borders, Mitred page 133.

14. Place the ground fabric right side up on the pattern. In pencil, mark a broken line down the center of the vine for placement of the bias tube. See Border Patterns page 20. NOTE: Move the pattern as needed to finish entire border strip.

15. Starting 18″ from one corner, pin flowers, stems, leaves, and centers in place. Pin bias tube in place following the drawn line.

16. Starting on an outer curve, appliqué bias tube in place. NOTE: Tuck under stem of flower and leaves, folding 3⁄16″ seam allowance on each side of the motifs as you reach them. Leave raw edges flat under bias vine.

17. You may appliqué the entire vine, then flowers, stem, and leaves or you may appliqué some of each as you go—a little vine, a stem, a leaf, a flower. NOTE: Appliqué to within 18″ of the corners on all border strips.

18. Continue in this manner, following steps 14–17 until all four borders are completed.

19. Add border to quilt top.

20. When corners are mitred, complete the appliqué of the vine, leaves, and flowers.

21. Press borders following instructions in Pressing page 128.

To finish the quilt, see Finishing, chapter 13, for instructions on pressing the completed quilt top, preparing the batting, preparing the backing, assembling the three layers, quilting (see quilting pattern on page 201), and binding.

Side triangle   Corner triangle

Baltimore Album Quilt, *appliquéd and quilted by Wendy Cowan*

In the summer of 1978 Janet Carruth and I traveled for six weeks across the country from New York to Arizona. We were accompanied by Janet's four-year-old daughter, Kelly. Our days were filled with visits to quilt shops, living museums, McDonald's restaurants, and antique stores—as well as traveling to the next city on the agenda. In Washington, D.C., we attended the first National Quilt Congress, an exciting event with classes, lectures, exhibits, and a merchant mall. In a booth in the merchant mall, we met Elly Sienkiewicz. Elly has an enormous interest in history, especially the history of quilts in the area surrounding her home city of Washington, D.C. The *Baltimore Album* quilts, resplendent with color and fine appliqué chronicling the events of the 1840s through the 1850s, have become her forte. In the late 1980s, Elly taught workshops at The Quilted Apple, sharing her love of the album quilts and some of the techniques needed to make them. The students in those workshops wanted more, so I began to teach more techniques with more patterns. The first patterns came from Elly, but then I had to research and draft patterns to keep ahead of my students. And what began as a small group of inexperienced appliquérs has grown to hundreds of avid and excellent needleworkers with beautiful blocks and quilts.

The block in the center of this wall quilt is in the *Friendship Album Quilt,* shown on page 8, made for me by students and staff at The Quilted Apple. The block pattern, taken from a *Baltimore Album Quilt* dated 1846 and discovered in Prescott, Arizona, is similar to those on many album quilts of that era. A bowl with fruit and foliage fills the block. I designed the border to define and add beauty to the center block; it contains fruit on an undulating vine. Wendy Cowan, from Glendale, Arizona, appliquéd and quilted this wall quilt. (In my large quilt Wendy appliquéd the block with the bird above the lyre in the floral wreath.) Her appliqué and quilting are magnificent, and her love of the work is obvious in the block on my quilt and in this wall quilt.

All of the motifs are large and will not be difficult to appliqué. Your choice of fabrics for the bowl and fruit will add a new flavor to this antique design. Go for it and enjoy!

The quilting designs are simple and add to the beauty of the appliqué. Wendy has crosshatched, one-half inch apart, the ground of the center block She outline-quilted the border motifs and echo-quilted the undulating vine. A splendid finish for a beautiful wall quilt.

BALTIMORE ALBUM QUILT

STITCHING TECHNIQUE	Tack
SETTING	Straight set
FABRIC SUGGESTIONS	
Ground, border, and backing	Off-white solid
Inner border and binding	Red print
Bowl	Blue print
All fruits and foliage	Prints in appropriate colors
FINISHED SIZE	34″ × 34″
FINISHED BLOCK SIZE	18″ × 18″

YARDAGE

GROUND, BORDER, AND BACKING	3
INNER BORDER AND BINDING	¾
MOTIFS	
Bowl	¼
Fruit	⅛ to ¼ each
Foliage	½
Vine, bias tube	½
BATTING	38″ × 38″

CUTTING

GROUND	
Block	20″ × 20″
MOTIFS	
Fruits and foliage	As needed for block and border (see Template Patterns)
BIAS TUBE	1″
INNER BORDER WIDTH	1″
OUTER BORDER WIDTH	8″
BACKING	38″ × 38″
BINDING WIDTH	1½″

CONSTRUCTION

1. Prepare block pattern. See Pattern Preparation page 20.

2. Prepare templates. See About Templates page 20. Also see Template Patterns in the back of the book.

3. Prepare fabric motif shapes using one of the methods detailed in Essentials. Add ³⁄₁₆″ seam allowance to motifs. Prepare ¼″ bias tube. See Bias Preparation page 23.

4. Center ground fabric block right side up on pattern and pin fabric motif shapes in place.

5. Begin with the bowl. Using your round wooden toothpick, turn under seam allowance on the bottom of the bowl. Appliqué, using the tack stitch. NOTE: As you reach the leaves, fold under ³⁄₁₆″ seam allowance on leaf edges to fit under base of bowl. Do not appliqué end of leaf that is under base of bowl; leave the edge flat.

6. Continue the appliqué around the bowl. NOTE: As you reach the inner curves, you must clip to the drawn line as described in Stitches page 32.

7. Set your work down often on a flat surface and smooth it to prevent puckering.

8. Continue the appliqué, working with the fruit motifs. As they are appliquéd, take care to stitch the motifs in the background of the block first and layer the motifs in the foreground on top for a three-dimensional appearance. Consult instructions for corners, points, and circles in Tack Stitch page 30.

9. Trim the finished block to 18½″ × 18½″, centering design. Press block following instructions in Finishing page 128.

10. Prepare the border pattern by cutting two 7½″ × 26″ strips of butcher paper. Tape them together to form a corner. Trace the design onto the paper.

11. Cut inner and outer border fabric. See Borders, Mitred page 133. Place ground fabric border strip right side up on pattern and mark in pencil a broken line down the center of the vine for the placement of bias tube. NOTE: Move pattern as needed to finish entire border strip. See Border Patterns page 20.

12. Pin fabric motifs in place. Pin bias following the drawn line. NOTE: Tuck under leaves and stems when indicated on pattern.

13. You may appliqué the vine, then the leaves, and the fruit or you may appliqué some of each as you go — a little vine, leaves, and fruit, and so on. NOTE: Appliqué to within 8″ of the corners on all border strips.

14. Press border strips following instructions in Finishing page 128.

15. Stitch inner border strips and outer border strips together matching centers. Add borders to quilt top and mitre corners. See page 133.

16. When borders are mitred, complete the appliqué.

17. Press border corners. See Finishing page 128.

To finish the quilt, see Finishing, chapter 13, for information about pressing the completed quilt, preparing batting, preparing backing, assembling three layers, quilting, and binding.

PLACEMENT DIAGRAM

Chapter 12

~

TWENTIETH-CENTURY TRADITIONAL APPLIQUÉ

MOST OF US RECOGNIZE THE PIECED QUILT STYLES OF THE 1920S AND 1930S: *Double Wedding Ring, Dresden Plate,* and *Grandmother's Flower Garden.* However, we may not recognize the appliqué quilts of that era. Many of them were kits produced and sold by various companies. The fabrics usually help us to date the quilts if the designs do not.

I designed the *Easter Lily Quilt* using an antique block as the inspiration. Everyone comments favorably on the color combination. I hope you like it, also.

I am also including an antique quilt from a private collection; it is a *Bird of Paradise in Oak Leaf Cluster Quilt.* I had planned to use it in the Nineteenth-Century Traditional Appliqué chapter because, from the photo and slide, it looked to be from that era. Not so. See what you think. The bold design and the fabric colors are very deceiving.

Emma Andres, an Arizona quiltmaker of the 1930s and 1940s, wrote and received many letters a month from all over the United States. Emma enjoyed a fifteen-year correspondence with Carrie A. Hall, a renowned quilt expert, author, and lecturer. They wrote to each other weekly, sharing the mundane and exciting happenings of their lives.

Carrie Hall determined early in her quiltmaking career that she would be unable to make all the quilts she wanted to. So she began to make just one block of each pattern. The Thayer Museum of Art at the University of Kansas has the collection of over one thousand blocks, or patches as she called them. She included seven hundred of them in *Romance of the Patchwork Quilt in America,* published in 1935 and coauthored with Ruth Kretsinger.

In 1942 Carrie sent Emma an appliquéd block she had made specifically for her. The block, *Easter Lily,* designed by Harold Fisher, is no. 6 on page 118 of her book. It is pictured here just as it appears in Emma's scrapbook, with Scotch tape holding it to the page. The tape has long since marred the edges of the block but you will have no problem recognizing Carrie's fine appliqué, done some fifty years ago.

The block is unique because of the narrow bias edge on the two center petals. I have designed a quilt using this block design and added a flower with two petals in each of the scallops in the border. The fabrics are solids, and I changed only one color from Carrie's original. The narrow bias edge is now pink. It is an absolutely beautiful quilt.

The appliqué was done by Linda Callahan, a prize-winning master appliqué artist from Phoenix, Arizona. Linda was enthusiastic about doing the appliqué. She loved the tiny bias edge!

EASTER LILY QUILT

STITCHING TECHNIQUES	Tack, ladder
SETTING	Straight set with sashing and corner squares
FABRIC SUGGESTIONS	
Ground: blocks, border, and backing	Light blue
Flower centers, calyxes, and leaves	Green
Sashing and flower petals	Off-white
Sashing corner sets, bias, and binding	Pink

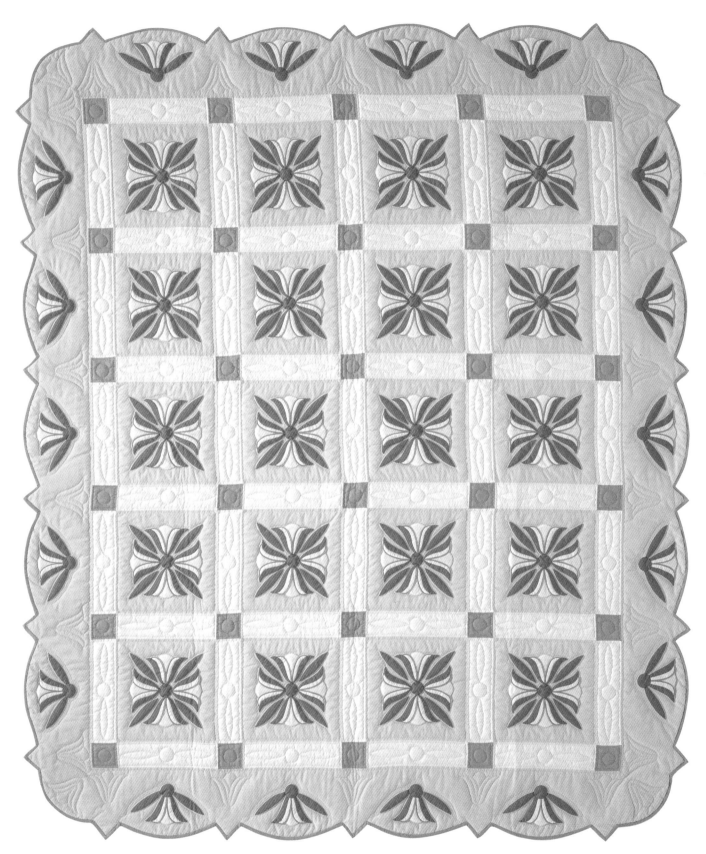

Easter Lily Quilt, *appliquéd by Linda Callahan and quilted by Una Jarvis*

	TWIN	DOUBLE/QUEEN	KING
FINISHED SIZE	70″ × 83″	83″ × 96″	96″ × 96″
BLOCKS SET	4 × 5	5 × 6	6 × 6
10″ × 10″ BLOCKS	20	30	36

YARDAGE

	TWIN	DOUBLE/QUEEN	KING
GROUND			
Blocks and borders	4	5½	6
FLOWER CENTERS, CALYXES, AND LEAVES	2	2⅓	3
SASHING AND FLOWER PETALS	2¾	4	4½
SASHING CORNER SETS, BIAS, AND BINDING	2⅓	2⅔	2⅔
BACKING	5	5½	8½
BATTING	74″ × 87″	87″ × 100″	100″ × 100″

CUTTING

	TWIN	DOUBLE/QUEEN	KING
GROUND			
Blocks 12″ × 12″	20	30	36
MOTIFS			
Flower petals	294	426	504
Flower bias	¾″	¾″	¾″
Flower centers	38	52	60
Flowers calyxes	196	284	336
Leaves	116	164	192
SASHING 3½″ × 10½″	49	66	84
CORNER SQUARES 3½″ × 3½″	30	36	42
BORDER WIDTH	8″	8″	8″
BACKING LENGTHS	2	2	3
BIAS BINDING WIDTH (1½″)	20 yds.	23 yds.	25 yds.

CONSTRUCTION

1. Prepare a block pattern. See Pattern Preparation page 20.

2. Prepare templates. See About Templates page 20. Also see patterns in the back of the book.

3. Prepare fabric shapes using one of the methods detailed in Essentials. REMEMBER: Add 3/16″ seam allowance as you cut the fabric.

4. Prepare bias strip. See Bias Preparation page 23. Cut the bias ¾″ wide, fold in half, and press.

5. Center one block of ground fabric right side up on pattern, and pin fabric motif shapes in place on ground fabric.

QUILTING DIAGRAM

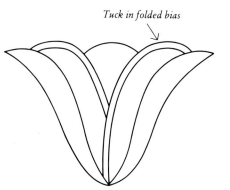

Tuck in folded bias

DIAGRAM 1

6. Using a round wooden toothpick, turn under seam allowance of the white flower center petal curve and appliqué using tack or ladder stitch. NOTE: Do *not* appliqué the area of the center that is under the two side petals. Leave edges flat.

7. Tuck the folded bias between the center and side flower petals. Fold under seam allowance on the petals and appliqué them in place, stitching through bias and ground. *(See diagram 1.)*

8. Appliqué the green calyxes in place.

9. Continue, following steps 6–8 to finish flowers.

10. Appliqué the green center and leaves. See Circles page 32.

11. Trim block to 10½″ × 10½″, centering design. Press block following instructions in Finishing page 128.

12. Continue in this manner, following steps 5–11 until all blocks are completed.

13. Prepare border pattern cutting two 7½″ × 30″ strips of butcher paper. Tape them together to form a corner. Trace the design onto the paper.

14. Cut borders; see Borders, Mitred page 133. Place ground fabric border strip right side up on pattern and pin motifs in place.

15. Appliqué flowers and leaves following steps 6–8 and 10 to complete 4 borders. Press the borders.

To finish the quilt, see Finishing, chapter 13, for instructions on setting blocks, sashings, and corners together (see Straight Set with Sashing and Corner Squares page 129), adding borders (see Borders, Scalloped page 134), preparing batting, preparing backing, assembling three layers, quilting (see quilting pattern page 214), and binding (see Curved Edges page 138).

BIRD OF PARADISE IN OAK LEAF CLUSTER QUILT

I love the bird designs found in many of the midnineteenth-century quilts. When I first saw a photograph of this *Bird of Paradise in Oak Leaf Cluster Quilt* I thought it was from that era. When I discovered it was made in Maryland, circa 1925–1930, I was surprised. When I saw the actual quilt, I realized the fabrics were obviously from the twentieth century.

In an era of numerous flowery quilt kits, the stylized design of this quilt must have been a bit out of place. The colors are bright—blue, red, and green. The design and colors recall an earlier time.

The appliqué will not be difficult. The tail is layered. The entire ground of the quilt is quilted in one-inch diagonal cross-hatching. Each motif is outline-quilted one-sixteenth of an inch from the edge of the appliqué.

All the fabrics in this quilt are solids. But you may wish to use some of the beautiful prints that are now available. Imagine a large print in shades of green as the leaves. The many red prints available could certainly be used for the wings, tail, and blossoms and will add a new dimension to the quilt. Take your time choosing the fabrics until you find just the perfect combination.

BIRD OF PARADISE IN OAK LEAF CLUSTER QUILT

STITCHING TECHNIQUES	Tack, ladder
SETTING	Straight set
FABRIC SUGGESTIONS	
Ground	Off-white solid
Motifs	Red, orange, blue, brown, green, and white solids
Backing	Off-white solid
Binding	Off-white solid

	TWIN	DOUBLE/QUEEN	KING
FINISHED SIZE	66″ × 77″	88″ × 99″	110″ × 121″
BLOCKS SET	2 × 3	3 × 4	4 × 5
22″ × 22″ BLOCKS	6	12	20

Bird of Paradise in Oak Leaf Cluster Quilt, *courtesy of The Ardis & Robert James Collection*

YARDAGE

	TWIN	DOUBLE/QUEEN	KING
GROUND:			
Blocks and borders	4⅔	7	10½
MOTIFS			
Blue	3	4½	6¾
Brown	¾	1	1
Red	¾	1¼	1¾
Orange	½	1	1¼
Green	¼	¼	½
White	⅛	⅛	⅛
BACKING	5	6	10⅔
BATTING	70″ × 81″	92″ × 103″	114″ × 125″
BINDING	¾	1	1

CUTTING

	TWIN	DOUBLE/QUEEN	KING
GROUND			
Blocks 24″ × 24″	6	12	20
LEAVES AND BRANCHES			
Leaves A, B, C, D, and E—Blue	6 each	12 each	20 each
Branch F—Blue	6	12	20
Branch G—Brown	6	12	20
BUDS			
Small red	18	36	60
Small orange	6	12	20
Large red	6	12	20
Large orange	6	12	20
BIRD			
Head			
Red	6	12	20
Orange	6	12	20
Body			
Green	6	12	20
White	6	12	20
Wings			
Red	12	24	40
Orange	6	12	20
Tail			
Red	6	12	20
Orange	6	12	20
BORDER MOTIFS			
Branch—piece as necessary			
Leaves	36	48	60

Buds			
Small red	16	28	40
Small orange	18	30	42
BORDER WIDTH (sides and bottom only)	11½″	11½″	11½″
BACKING LENGTHS	2	2	3
BINDING WIDTH	1½″	1½″	1½″

CONSTRUCTION

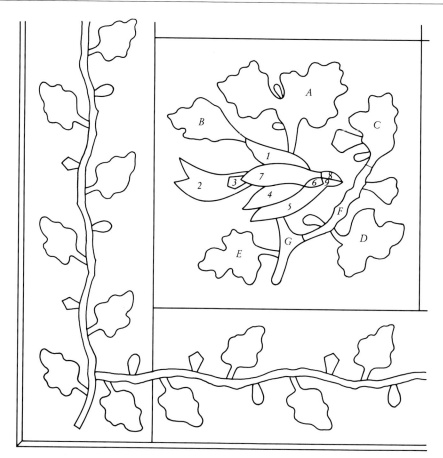

1. Prepare one large block pattern. See Pattern Preparation page 20.

2. Prepare templates. See About Templates page 20. See Template Patterns in the back of the book.

3. Prepare fabric shapes using one of the methods detailed in Essentials.

4. Center one block of ground fabric right side up on the pattern and pin fabric motif shapes in place.

5. Using a round wooden toothpick, turn under seam allowance, and start the appliqué on the outer curve of wing no. 1 at the junction of the wing and body using tack or ladder stitch. NOTE: As you come to the leaf, fold under 3⁄16″ seam allowance to fit under wing. Do not appliqué area of wing that is under the body. Leave the edge flat.

6. Set your work down often on a flat surface and smooth it to prevent puckering.

7. Continue the appliqué in the following order:
- Tail no. 2 and no. 3 under body no. 7.
- Inner wing no. 4 under body no. 7 and under outer wing no. 5.
- White neck area no. 6 under all remaining pieces.
- Body no. 7 under head no. 8 and no. 9, over tail no. 2 and no. 3, and over white neck area no. 6.
- Lower wing no. 5 over inner wing no. 4, branch, and white neck area no. 6.
- Lower head no. 9 over white neck area no. 6.
- Upper head no. 8 over white neck area no. 6 and body no. 7.

8. Appliqué leaves, tree branches, and buds.

9. Trim block to 22½″ × 22½″, centering design. Press block following instructions in Finishing page 128.

10. Continue in this manner, following steps 4–9, until all blocks are complete.

11. Set blocks together. See Straight Set page 128.

12. Cut and attach squared borders to quilt top. See Borders, Squared page 132. NOTE: The pattern calls only for side and bottom borders. If you want to attach a top border, do so at this time.

13. Prepare border pattern by cutting two 11″ × 36″ strips of butcher paper. Tape them together to form corner. Trace the design onto the paper.

14. Place ground fabric border strip right side up on pattern. Use a pencil to mark a broken line down the center of the branch for placement. See Border Patterns page 20. NOTE: Move pattern and adjust as needed to finish entire border. Use the photo as guide.

15. Pin leaves and buds in place. Pin branch motif following drawn line. Turn under seam allowance, and appliqué in place. NOTE: Tuck the leaves and buds under the branch.

To finish the quilt, see Finishing, chapter 13, for instructions on pressing the completed quilt top, preparing the batting, preparing the backing, assembling three layers, quilting, and binding.

Chapter 13

~

FINISHING

PRESSING

APPLIQUÉD BLOCKS AND BORDER STRIPS

1. Place a heavy terry cloth towel on the ironing board. NOTE: The soft toweling will prevent appliqué motif seam allowances from showing through to the right side of the pressed piece.

2. Place the right side of the block or border face down on towel.

3. Place a pressing cloth on top of block to prevent iron point from catching on threads. NOTE: I use one of my husband's white handkerchiefs for a pressing cloth. Pieces of an old sheet work well too.

4. Steam press so the ground and appliqué motifs are smooth and wrinkle free. NOTE: I sometimes lightly dampen the pressing cloth on particularly wrinkled areas.

SETTING BLOCKS TOGETHER

STRAIGHT SET

1. Place the blocks, in the order they will appear in your quilt, on a flat surface. NOTE: Your blocks should be pressed and trimmed to exact size, including seam allowances, before you begin.

2. Pin the right sides of the blocks together and machine stitch with a ¼″ seam allowance. *(See diagram 1.)*

3. When a full row is stitched, press all seam allowances in the same direction. Press next row's seam allowances in the opposite direction. *(See diagram 2.)*

DIAGRAM 1

4. Continue in this manner until all rows are completed. NOTE: Alternating the direction of the seam allowance prevents bulk in the corners and creates a much easier final assembly.

5. Pin 2 rows together matching seams, easing as necessary so they fit perfectly. Stitch. *(See diagram 3.)*

6. Continue in this manner until top is completed. *(See diagram 4.)*

STRAIGHT SET WITH SASHING

1. Place the blocks and short sashing strips, as they will be in your quilt, on a flat surface. NOTE: Your blocks should be pressed and trimmed to exact size, including seam allowances, before you begin.

2. Pin the blocks and short sashing strips right sides together in rows. At this point, be sure all strips are equal in length. Machine stitch using ¼" seam allowance.

3. Press the seam allowance into the sashing strips. *(See diagram 5.)*

4. Continue in this manner until all rows are completed.

5. Pin the right side of one row to the right side of a long sashing strip. Stitch using a ¼" seam allowance. *(See diagram 6.)*

6. Press the seam allowance into sashing strip. *(See diagram 7.)*

7. Continue in this manner until all rows are completed. *(See diagram 8.)*

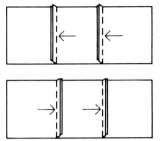

DIAGRAM 2

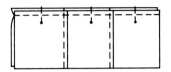

DIAGRAM 3

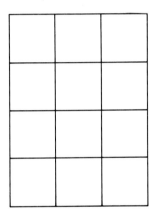

DIAGRAM 4

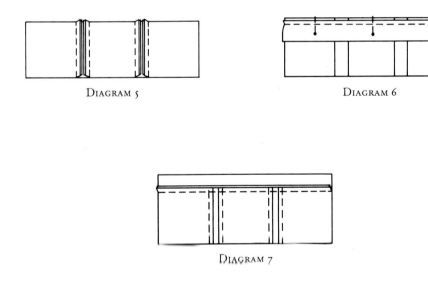

DIAGRAM 5

DIAGRAM 6

DIAGRAM 7

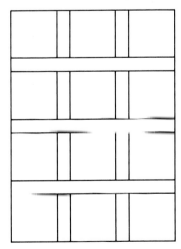

DIAGRAM 8

STRAIGHT SET WITH
SASHING AND CORNER SQUARES

1. Place the blocks and short sashing strips, as they will be in your quilt, on a flat surface. NOTE: Your blocks should be pressed and trimmed to exact size, including seam allowances, before you begin.

2. Pin the blocks and short sashing strips right sides together in rows. Machine stitch using a ¼" seam allowance.

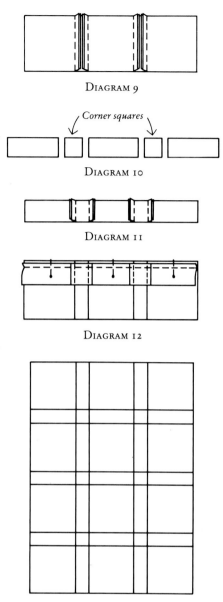

DIAGRAM 9

Corner squares

DIAGRAM 10

DIAGRAM 11

DIAGRAM 12

DIAGRAM 13

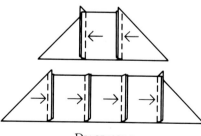

DIAGRAM 14

DIAGRAM 15

3. Press the seam allowance into sashing strips. *(See diagram 9.)*

4. Continue in this manner until all rows are completed, making sure all strips are equal in length.

5. To form long rows of sashing, stitch the corner squares to the short sashing strips. *(See diagram 10.)*

6. Press the seam allowance away from the corner pieces. *(See diagram 11.)*

7. Pin the right side of a row of blocks and sashing to right side of a long sashing and corner squares strip, matching all the seams. Stitch. *(See diagram 12.)*

8. Continue in this manner until all rows are completed. *(See diagram 13.)*

DIAGONAL SET

1. Place the blocks, side triangles, and corner triangles, in the order they will be in your quilt, on a flat surface. NOTE: Your blocks should be pressed and trimmed to exact size, including seam allowances, before you begin.

2. Pin the triangles and blocks right sides together in rows. Stitch using ¼″ seam allowance.

3. When one row is stitched, press all the seam allowances in the same direction. Press next row's seam allowances in opposite direction. *(See diagram 14.)*

4. Continue in this manner until all rows are completed. NOTE: Alternating the direction of the seam allowance prevents bulk in the corners and makes for a much easier final assembly.

5. Pin 2 rows together matching seams and easing as necessary so they fit perfectly. Machine stitch using ¼″ seam allowance. *(See diagram 15.)* NOTE: When attaching the corner triangles, find and match triangle centers to block centers for a perfect fit.

6. Continue in this manner until top is completed. *(See diagram 16.)* Stay stitch around quilt top to prevent sides from stretching.

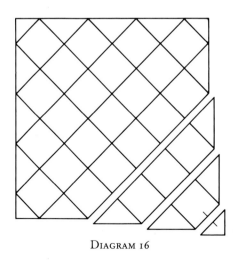

DIAGRAM 16

DIAGONAL SET WITH SASHING AS USED WITH SUNBONNET SUE

1. Place the blocks, short and long sashing strips, side triangles, and corner triangles, in the order they will appear in your quilt, on a flat surface. NOTE: Your blocks should be pressed and trimmed to exact size, including seam allowances, before you begin.

2. Pin short sashing strips and blocks right sides together in rows. Machine stitch using a ¼" seam allowance.

3. Press all seam allowances into the short sashing strips. *(See diagram 17.)*

4. Continue in this manner until all rows are completed.

5. Pin the right side of a row to the right side of a long sashing strip. Stitch.

6. Press seam allowance into the long sashing strips. *(See diagram 18.)*

7. Add side triangles using diagram 19 as a guide. Add corner triangles last.

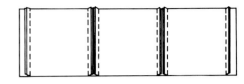

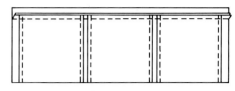

DIAGRAM 18

MEDALLION ON POINT

1. Trim center medallion to an exact square. Establish correct size for center block and borders as in step 2 of Borders, Mitred (page 133). Place the block, borders, and corner triangles, in the order they will be in your quilt top, on a flat surface. NOTE: Your blocks should be pressed and trimmed to exact size, including seam allowances, before you begin.

2. Fold fabric in half and finger press the lengthwise center points. *(See diagram 20.)*

DIAGRAM 19

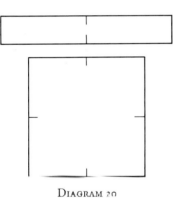

DIAGRAM 20

3. With right sides together and center points matching, pin a block to a border strip.

4. With the block on top, start stitching ¼" from the edge of the block; use a ¼" seam allowance. Stop ¼" from the end. *(See diagram 21.)*

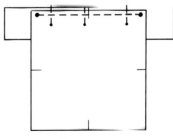

DIAGRAM 21

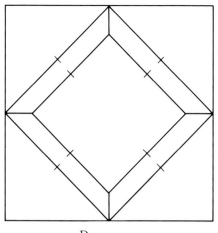

Diagram 22

5. Continue in this manner, following steps 2–4, until all inner border strips are attached.

6. Mitre border corners. See Borders page 133.

7. To add the corner triangles, fold them and the borders in half to find their center points. Finger press. Match these center points, pin, and sew in place. *(See diagram 22.)*

8. Add all outside border strips and mitre all corners. See Borders page 133.

9. Press all seam allowances into the border strips.

BORDERS

SQUARED

1. Measure across the center of your quilt top to determine length of top and bottom border strips. *(See diagram 23.)*

2. Cut 2 border strips the width listed in specific quilt requirements and the length you determine in step 1.

3. Find the center point of the top and bottom of the quilt top. Mark them with pins. Fold the border strips in half lengthwise. Mark the center points with pins. *(See diagram 24.)*

4. Pin border strips to the top and bottom of quilt, right sides together, matching center points. Ease in fullness if necessary. Stitch together using a ¼" seam allowance. *(See diagram 25.)*

5. Press seam allowance into border strips. See Pressing page 128.

6. Measure across center of your quilt top lengthwise to determine length of side borders. *(See diagram 26.)*

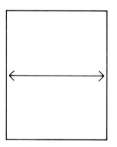

Diagram 23

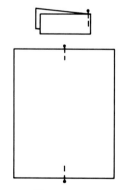

Diagram 24

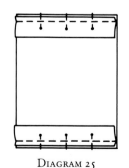

Diagram 25

Diagram 26

7. Cut 2 border strips the width in specific quilt requirements and the length you determine in step 6.

8. Find the center points of the sides of your quilt top. Mark these with pins. Fold border strips in half lengthwise, and mark these center points with pins.

9. Pin the border strips to the sides of the quilt top, right sides together, matching center points. Ease in fullness if necessary. Stitch. *(See diagram 27.)*

10. Press the seam allowance into border strips. *(See diagram 28.)*

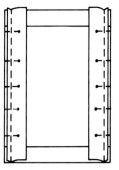

DIAGRAM 27

MITRED

1. Measure your quilt top across the center crosswise and lengthwise. *(See diagram 29.)*

2. Add double the width of the border, as listed in the specific quilt requirements, plus 2″ for mitre, to the crosswise measurements above.

FOR EXAMPLE: 52″ crosswise measurement

           12″ border width (6″ doubled)

       + 2″ for mitre

          66″ length of border

3. Repeat step 2 to determine the lengthwise measurement.

4. Cut the 4 border strips using the measurements determined in steps 2 and 3.

5. Find the center points of the top and bottom of the quilt top. Mark them with pins. Fold top and bottom border strips in half lengthwise to find the center points. Mark them with pins. *(See diagram 30.)*

6. Pin the border strips to the top and bottom of the quilt top, right sides together, matching center points. Ease in fullness if necessary. NOTE: Border fabrics will extend beyond the edges of quilt top.

7. Starting ¼″ from the corner of the quilt top, stitch the border using ¼″ seam allowance, ending ¼″ from the opposite corner of the quilt top. Secure beginning and ending stitches. NOTE: Do not stitch all the way to the edge of the quilt top. *(See diagram 31.)*

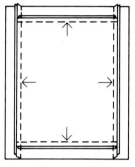

DIAGRAM 28

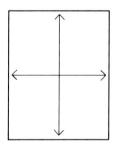

DIAGRAM 29

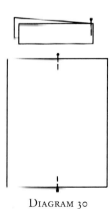

DIAGRAM 30

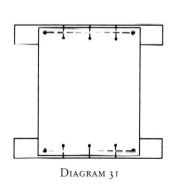

DIAGRAM 31

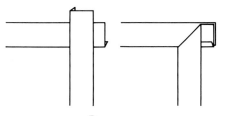

DIAGRAM 32

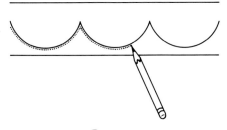

DIAGRAM 33

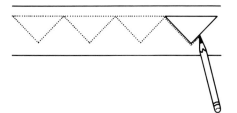

DIAGRAM 34

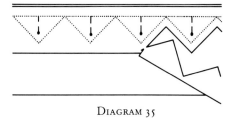

DIAGRAM 35

8. Continue in this manner following steps 5–7 until all 4 borders are attached. Press seam allowance into borders.

9. To mitre the corner by hand, fold a side border strip under itself at a 45-degree angle. This border strip's tail will now lie on top of adjacent border strip. *(See diagram 32.)*

    a. Press the fold and pin in place. Stitch the folded edge of the mitred corner with matching thread. Trim the seam allowance to ½″.

    b. Continue in this manner until all 4 corners are completed.

    c. Press seam allowance open.

10. To mitre the corner by machine, fold a side border strip under itself at a 45-degree angle. This border strip's tail will now lie on top of adjacent border strip.

    a. Press fold to crease. Turn quilt top to wrong side. Pin border strips in place near the pressed crease. Machine stitch exactly on creased line. Stitch from the inside corner to the outside edge. Trim seam allowance to ½″.

    b. Continue in this manner until all 4 corners are completed.

    c. Press mitred seams open.

SCALLOPED

1. Attach mitred borders. See Borders, Mitred, page 133.

2. Place the scalloped border template for your specific quilt on the right side of fabric. Mark the scalloped edge with a pencil. *(See diagram 33.)* Cut on drawn line. Assemble batting and backing. Quilt. See Curved Edges page 138 to attach binding.

SAWTOOTH OR DOG'S TOOTH

The triangles applied as an inner and/or outer edge of the border are known as sawtooth or dog's tooth edges. The sawtooth is a wider and shorter triangle; the dog's tooth is longer and narrower. An example of both styles appears in the *Star of Bethlehem with Broderie Perse* quilt.

1. Measure the length of the border strip. Divide that figure by the width of the finished triangle to determine the number of triangles needed.

2. For ease in placement of the triangles, draw a line ¼″ from the raw edge for a seam allowance. Place the triangle template on the right side of the fabric along the drawn line and trace around it. Now place the template next to the first drawn triangle and trace again. Continue until you have a strip of triangles the length of the border strip. *(See diagram 34.)* The strip may be pieced between triangles if your fabric is not long enough.

3. With raw edges even, place the triangle strip right side up on the right side of the border strip. Pin in place.

4. Cut out triangles, a few at a time, adding ³⁄₁₆″ seam allowance. *(See diagram 35.)* Appliqué in place.

BATTING

The antique quilts included in this book all have 100 percent cotton batting. Most of the quilts have been quilted heavily, and thin batting makes that easier.

We are fortunate to live in a time when many types and thicknesses of batts are available. Your local quilt shop will give you information and help concerning the different manufacturers and the features of each brand. The batt should extend at least two inches beyond all four sides of the quilt top. The yardage measurements include this allowance. You'll trim the excess after the quilting is completed.

BACKING

Choose 100 percent cotton solids or prints that combine well in color and design with your quilt top and that please you. The lengthwise grain line of the backing fabric should run the length of the quilt to keep the quilt straight through many washings. All the yardage measurements in this book are the length of the quilt by the number of widths it will take to make the backing. When two widths are needed, the second is cut in half lengthwise and sewn to either side of the center width. On larger quilts, three widths are used and are all cut to the same measurement and sewn together with two seams. One center seam is more vulnerable especially when the quilt is quite large.

ASSEMBLING THREE LAYERS

QUILTING IN A HOOP

1. Place backing fabric wrong side up on the floor or a large table. Tape four corners to the floor or table taking care to keep the edges straight and the piece square.

2. Gently unroll batting onto the backing fabric, smoothing out any creases. The batting will cover the entire backing. Keep all edges even and straight

3. Place your quilt top, right side up, on top of the batting. Match the corners. Smooth out any fullness.

4. With large needle and quilting thread, baste all three layers together using large running stitches. Your basting lines should radiate from the center and should be about 8″ apart at the outside edges of the quilt. *(See diagram 36.)*

5. Choose a hoop at least 14″ in diameter that is a comfortable size for you to handle.

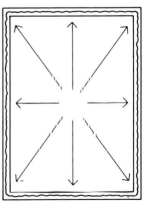

DIAGRAM 36

QUILTING IN A FRAME

Place backing fabric, batting, and quilt top into your quilting frame according to the manufacturer's instructions.

QUILTING DESIGNS

At The Quilted Apple we have several very fine quilters. Una Jarvis arrived just three weeks after we opened. She has quilted for us for almost fourteen years, working many hours every day in a room built especially for her quilting. Una loves appliqué quilts and she loves to quilt them. Why? Because they are so beautiful and because there are no seam allowances to quilt through.

The quilting around the appliqué motifs is done very close to the motif. It is almost, but not quite, in the ditch. Quilting on appliquéd quilts is not done ¼" from seam lines (as it is on pieced quilts) because the design must be given dimension. The quilting almost raises the motif from the ground fabric.

The beauty of a quilt is enhanced by the quilting. I have included patterns for some of the quilting designs found on the quilts. Many of the quilts have the following filler (area behind motif totally quilted) quilting patterns.

- *Cross-hatching:* Lines either diagonal or straight across a block or border equadistant apart. See *Baltimore Album Quilt* for an example of this.
- *Stippling:* Meandering or straight lines ⅟₁₆" to ⅛" apart. See *Pineapple Miniature Quilt* for an example of stippling.

ECHO QUILTING

Quilting around the appliquéd motif and then continuing to quilt multiple lines following the shape is called echo quilting. And it is aptly named because the quilting lines "echo" the shape.

In Hawaiian quilts the lines of quilting are the width of one "finger," as my friend Wailani taught me. NOTE: You may choose to echo quilt on any of your quilts. It does *not* have to be Hawaiian appliqué!

BINDING

The binding you choose for a quilt, wall quilt, or table topper is determined by the thickness of the batting and by whether the quilt has a straight or curved edge. Use bias binding on any quilt, including one with curved or zigzag edges. Use straight-cut binding on any quilt that doesn't have curved edges.

CUTTING BINDING

Cut straight binding strips on the true lengthwise or crosswise grain of the fabric following the width specified in the quilt you are making. Determine the length of binding needed as follows:

WITH SQUARED CORNERS: You will need to cut 4 strips of binding. The lengths used on the top and bottom should equal the lengths of the top and bottom of your quilt top. The sides will be a bit longer to give you enough extra binding to fold over the ends. Cut your side binding pieces the length of quilt top sides plus 2″.

WITH MITRED CORNERS: Measure around the outside edge of your quilt and add 10″. The binding will be attached to your quilt in one continuous piece.

WITH BIAS BINDING: See Continuous Strips for Bindings and Long Vines (page 24) for instructions on cutting bias. Measure around the outside edge of your quilt and add 10″. The binding will be attached to your quilt in one continuous strip.

SQUARED CORNERS

1. Trim batting and backing to within 1″ of quilt top. *(See diagram 37).*

2. Fold your quilt top in half to find the center of the top and bottom edges and finger press. Repeat with the binding. Match centers, pin, and stitch the binding in place (the edges of the binding should be flush to edges of quilt) using ¼″ seam.

3. Trim batting and backing even with the top and bottom.

4. Fold the binding to the back, turn under seam allowance, and hand stitch.

5. Find the centers of the quilt top sides and the side binding pieces. Match centers and pin in place; the binding will extend above and below the quilt top. Fold the extended binding over to the back and stitch through all layers.

6. Trim the batting and backing even with the sides.

7. Fold the binding to the back, turn under seam allowance, and hand stitch. Because you stitched through all layers in step 5, you should have perfect corners.

MITRED CORNERS

1. Trim batting and backing to within 1″ of quilt top. *(See diagram 37.)*

2. With right sides together, match the raw edge of the binding strip with raw edge of quilt top. Starting in the center of one side and ½″ from the end of the binding, stitch through binding, quilt top, batting, and backing using ¼″ seam allowance. Stop ¼″ from corner

3. Remove needle from quilt. Fold up binding, forming right angle, and hold it in place. *(See diagram 38.)*

4. Now, bring the binding down, with the raw edges matched to the next side. Start stitching at the top of the fold of the binding. Stitch through all layers. *(See diagram 39.)*

5. Continue around the quilt in this manner. When you reach the starting point, fold over the loose edge, overlay it with the end, and stitch.

6. Trim batting and backing even with the seam allowance.

7. Turn binding over the edge of the quilt to the back and hand stitch to the backing fabric. NOTE: Turn in the folds of binding to form the mitre. You may have to take a stitch or two to secure it.

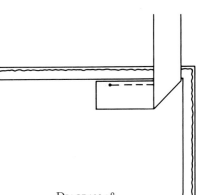

DIAGRAM 37   *Cut here*

DIAGRAM 38

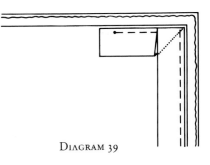

DIAGRAM 39

CURVED EDGES

1. Always use bias binding on curves. Prepare continuous bias. See page 24.

2. Do not trim batting or backing until you have sewn the binding in place. Match raw edges with right sides together. Stitch bias binding to quilt top. When you come to the dips in the scallops, sew to the point, keeping the needle in the fabric, pivot in the dip and realign edges to sew the next curve.

3. Trim batting and backing even with quilt top. Wrap binding over to the back of the quilt. A small tuck will form at each dip. Fold under a ¼″ seam allowance and hand stitch.

4. Smooth tucks evenly at each dip; stitch the folded edges of the tucks together. *(See diagram 40.)*

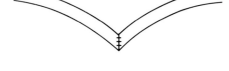

DIAGRAM 40

TEMPLATE PATTERNS

DIRECTIONS FOR ENLARGING ANY TEMPLATE PATTERNS SHOWN AT A REDUCED SIZE:

✪ FOR XEROX ENLARGEMENT — 50% reduction; xerox at 200%

25% reduction; xerox at 400%

✪ FOR RE-DRAFTING TEMPLATE PATTERN — each square on grid equals one inch

HAWAIIAN HEART BLOCK

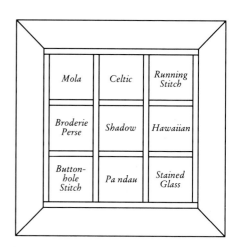

Mola	Celtic	Running Stitch
Broderie Perse	Shadow	Hawaiian
Button-hole Stitch	Pandau	Stained Glass

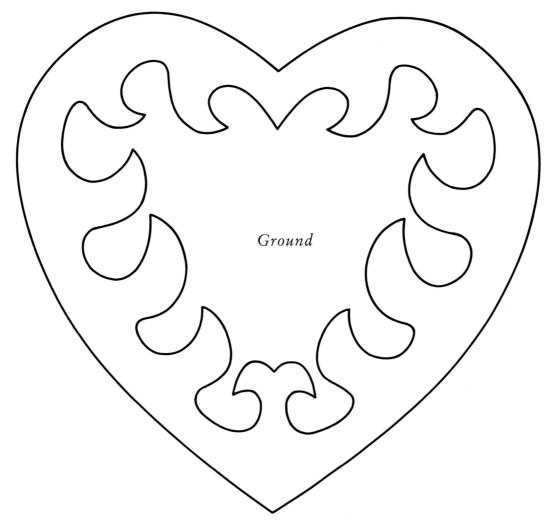

Ground

BRODERIE PERSE
HEART BLOCK

CELTIC HEART BLOCK

STAINED GLASS
HEART BLOCK

4

3

2

1

SHADOW HEART BLOCK

I

RUNNING STITCH
HEART BLOCK

1

2

3

4

BUTTONHOLE STITCH
HEART BLOCK

1

2

3

MOLA HEART BLOCK

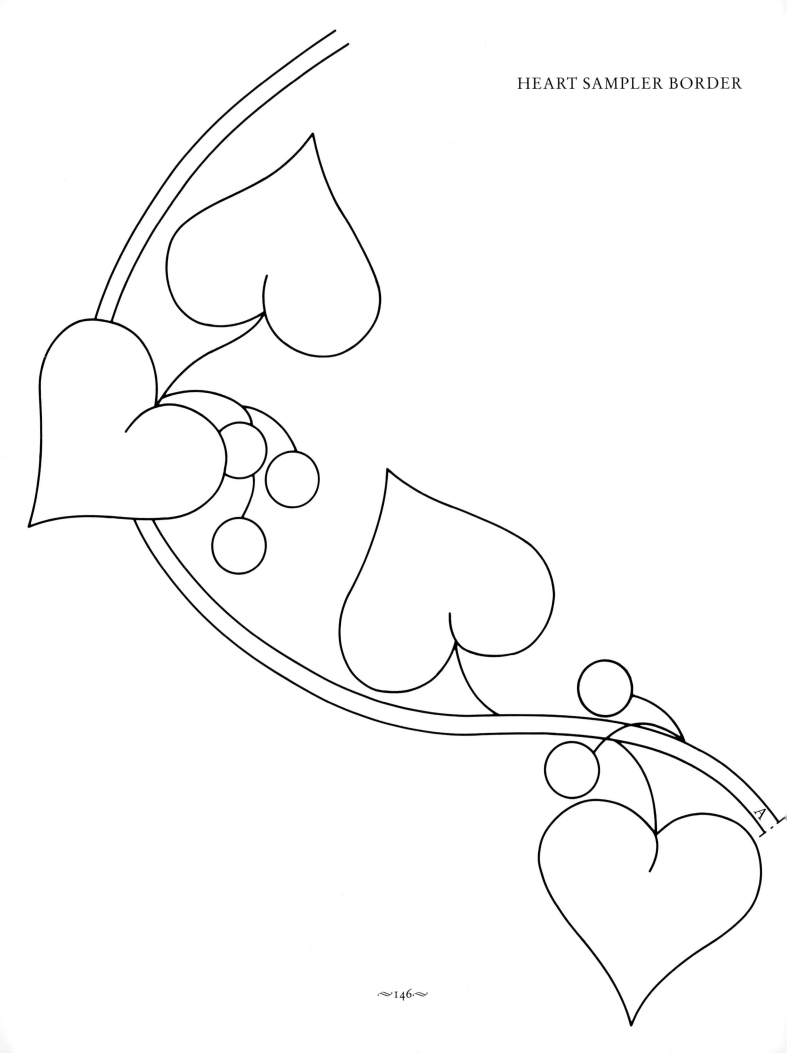

A.

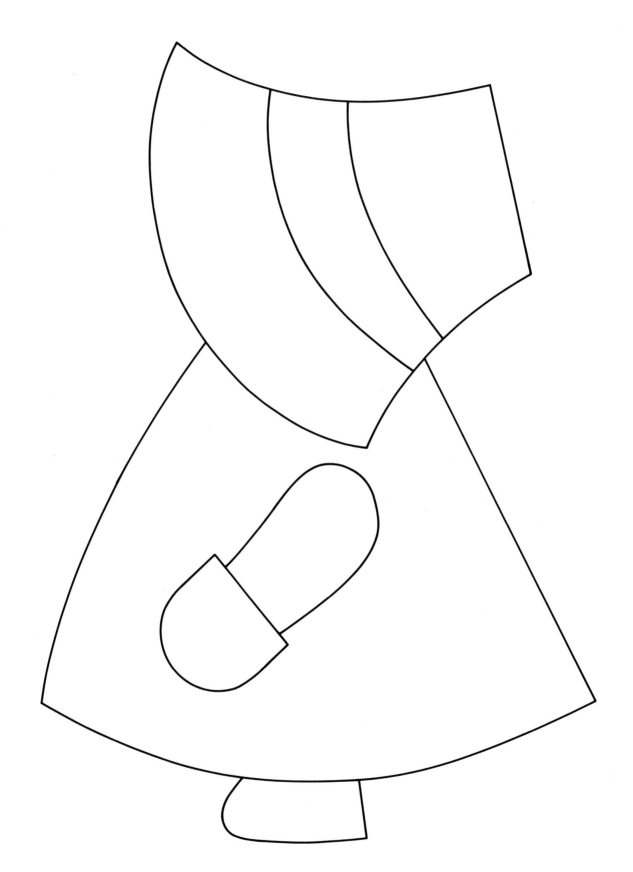

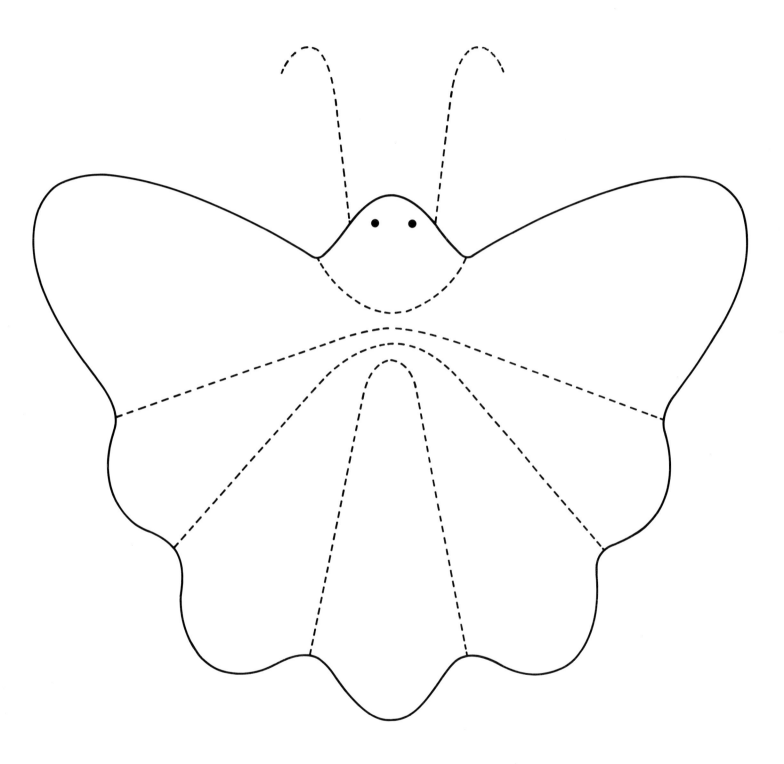

SUMMER CRADLE COVERLET

QUARTER OF BLOCK

Template pattern shown at 50% of finished size

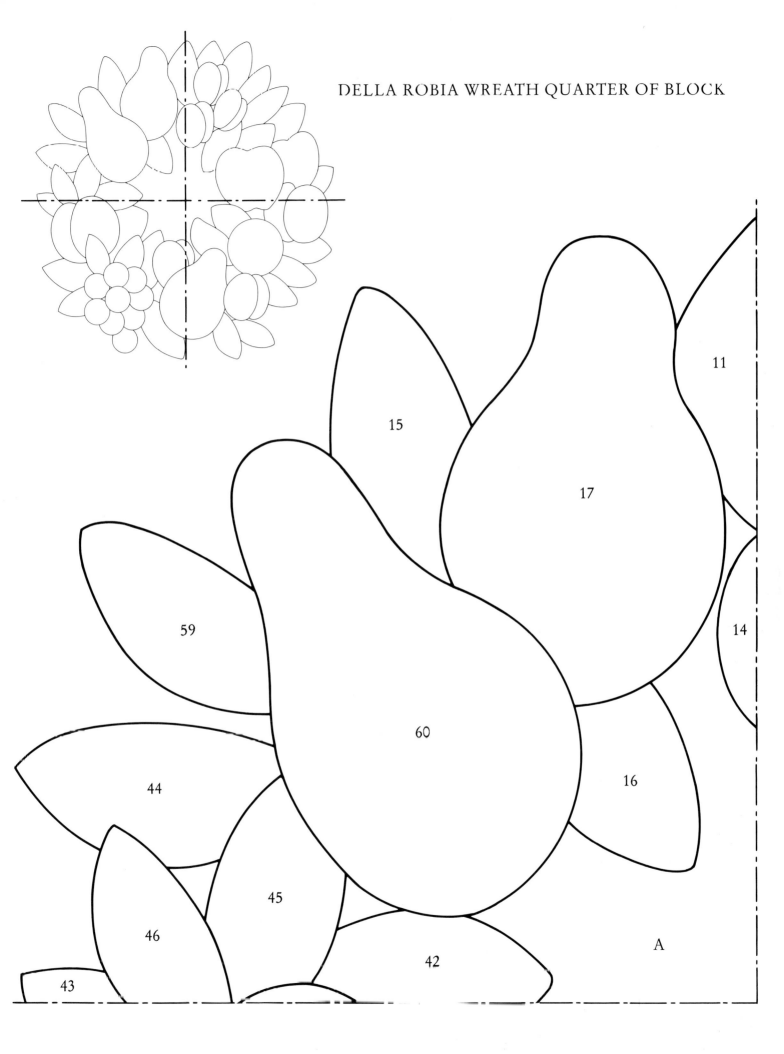

DELLA ROBIA WREATH QUARTER OF BLOCK

11

15

17

14

59

60

16

44

45

46

42

43

A

DELLA ROBIA WREATH QUARTER OF BLOCK

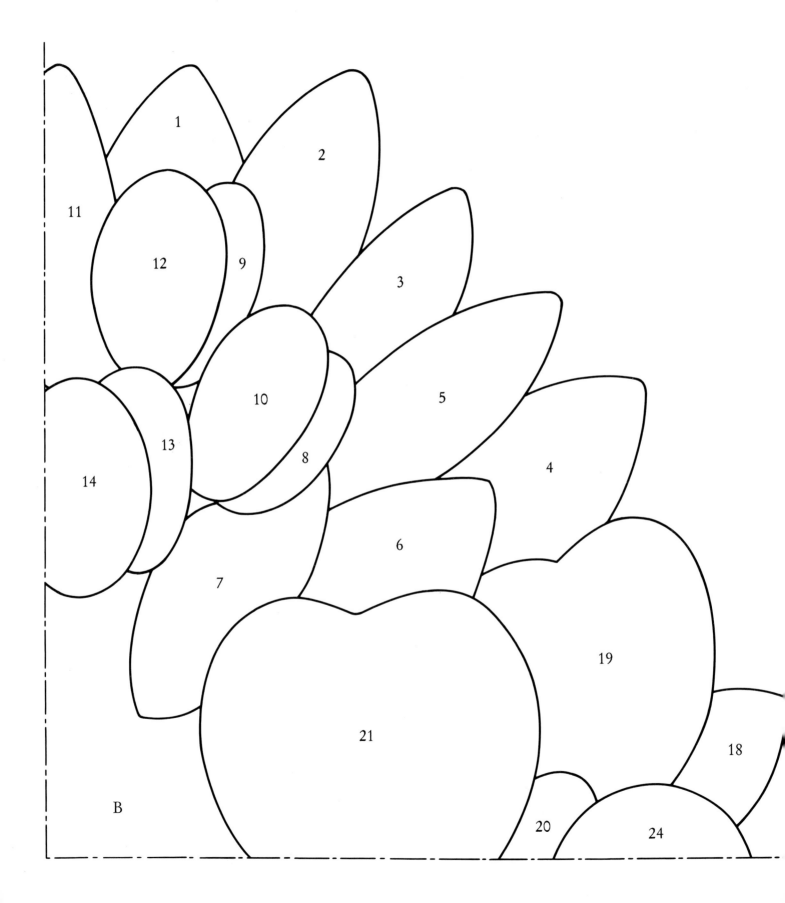

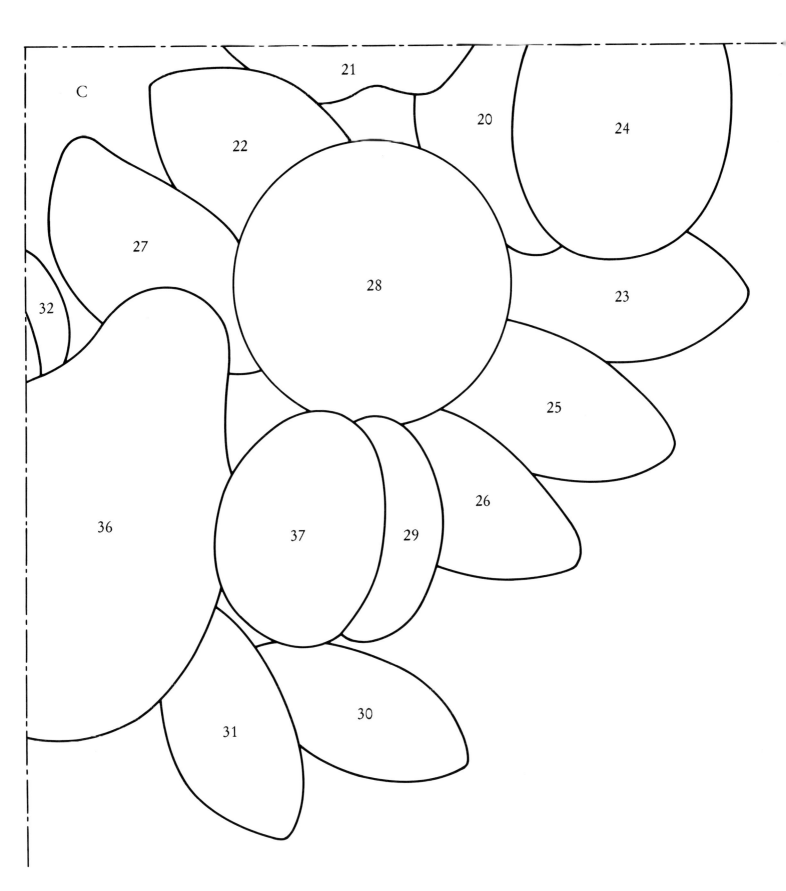

C

21

22

20

24

27

28

23

32

25

36

37 29 26

30

31

DELLA ROBIA WREATH QUARTER OF BLOCK

CELTIC BLOCK

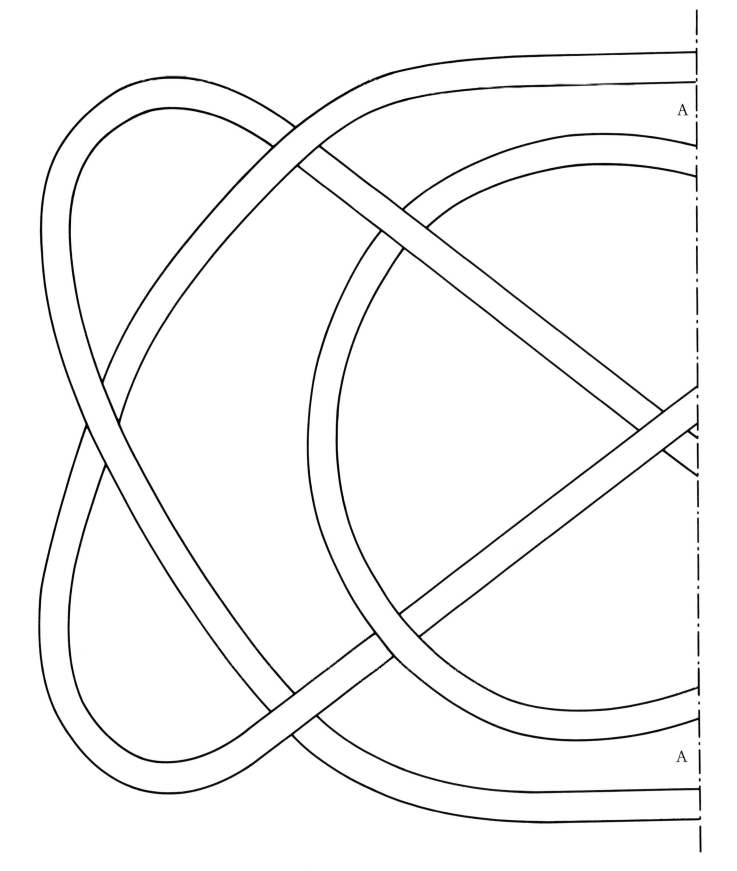

A

A

CELTIC BLOCK

A

B

A

B

CELTIC BLOCK

B

B

(To create complete pattern, make two and tape together here.)

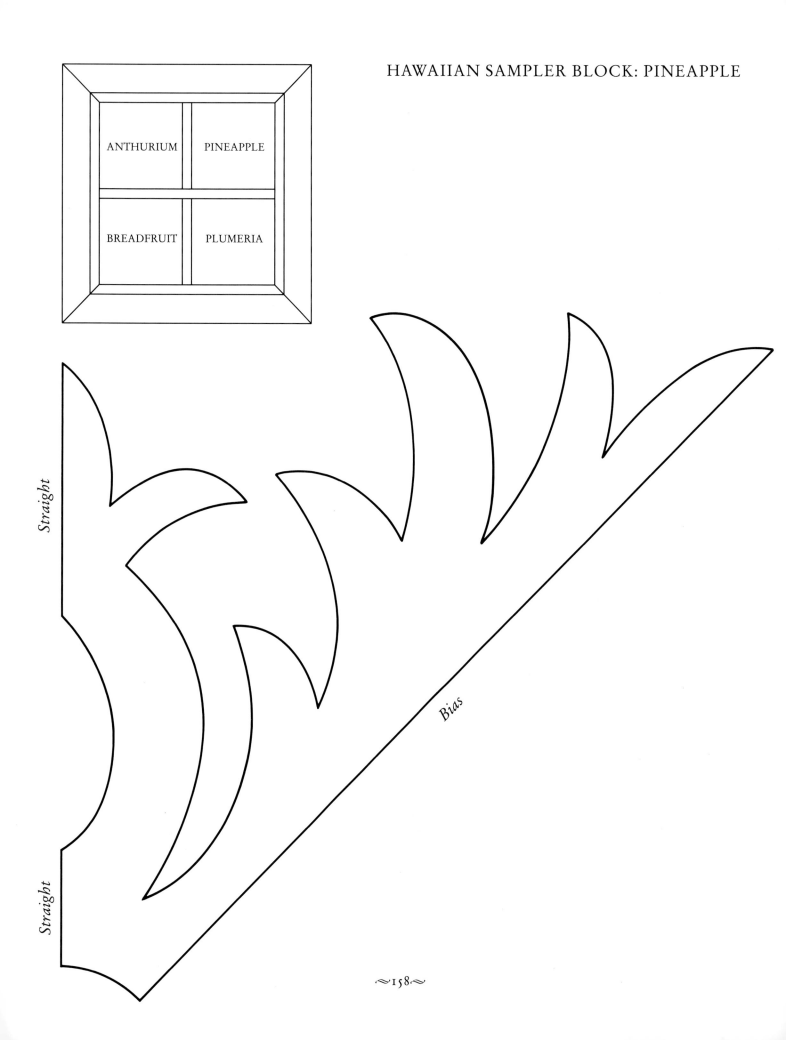

HAWAIIAN SAMPLER BLOCK: PINEAPPLE

ANTHURIUM	PINEAPPLE
BREADFRUIT	PLUMERIA

Straight

Straight

Bias

~158~

Straight

Bias

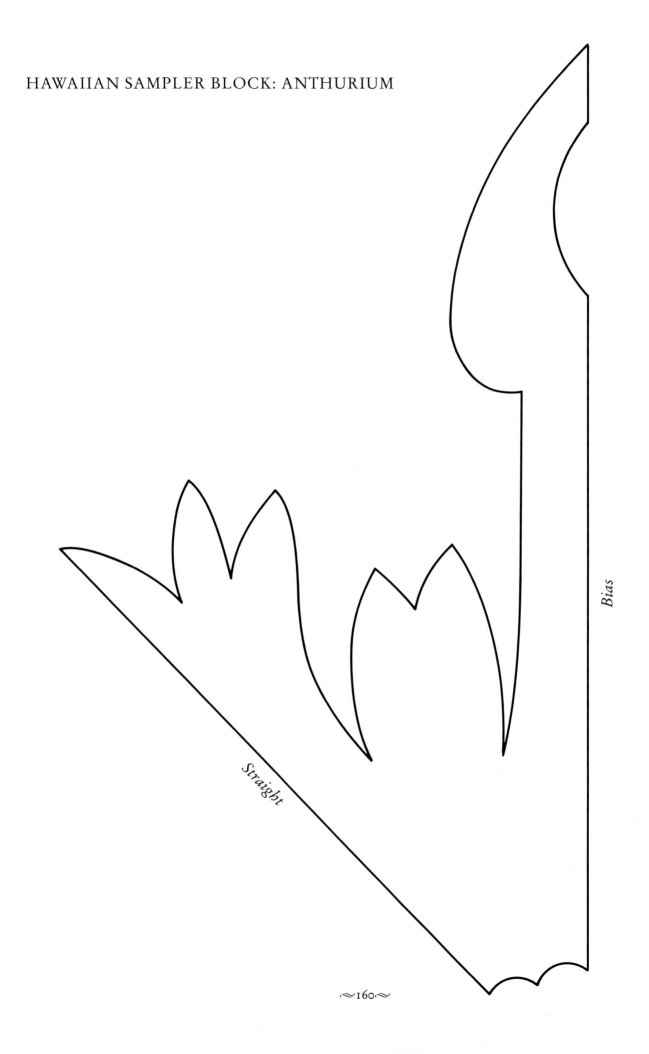

HAWAIIAN SAMPLER BLOCK: ANTHURIUM

Bias

Straight

Bias

Straight

HAWAIIAN QUILT CORNER MOTIF

Bias

A

Template pattern shown at 50% of finished size

A

Template pattern shown at 50% of finished size

*Template pattern shown at
50% of finished size*

Straight

A

A

Straight

B

Bias

Bias

B

Template pattern shown at 50% of finished size

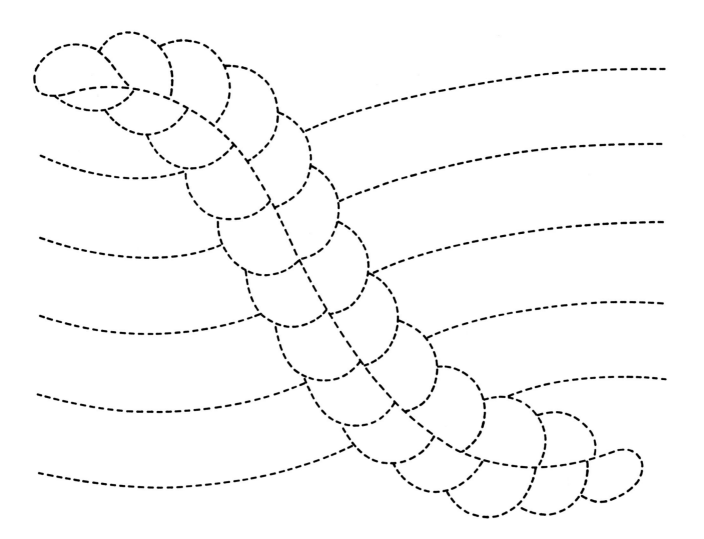

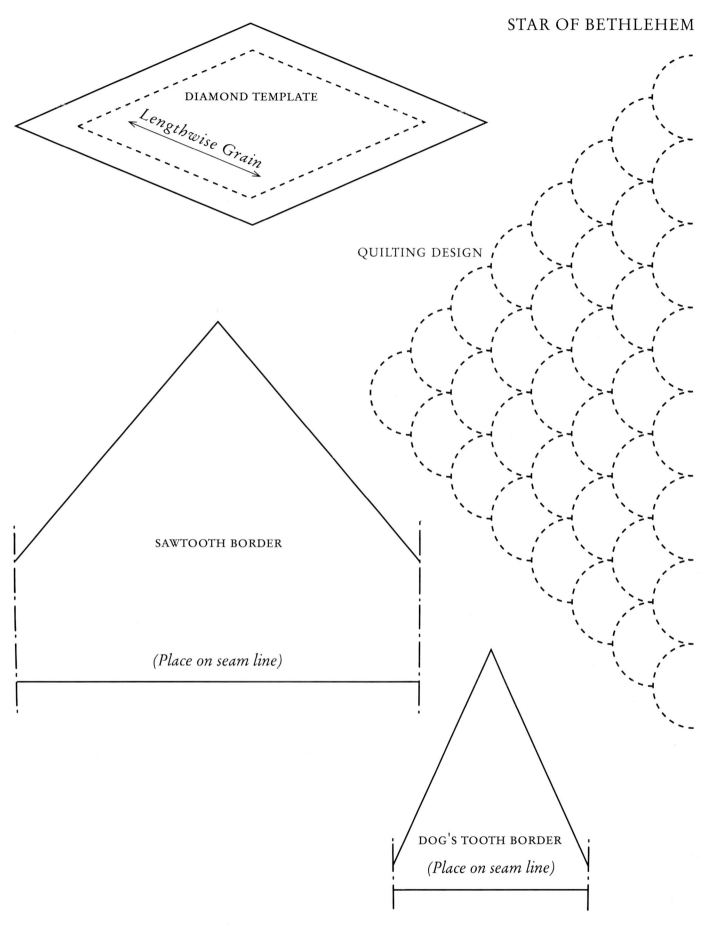

DIAMOND TEMPLATE

Lengthwise Grain

QUILTING DESIGN

SAWTOOTH BORDER

(Place on seam line)

DOG'S TOOTH BORDER

(Place on seam line)

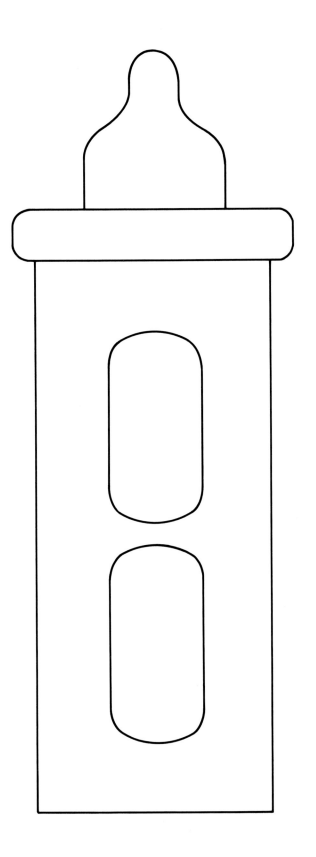

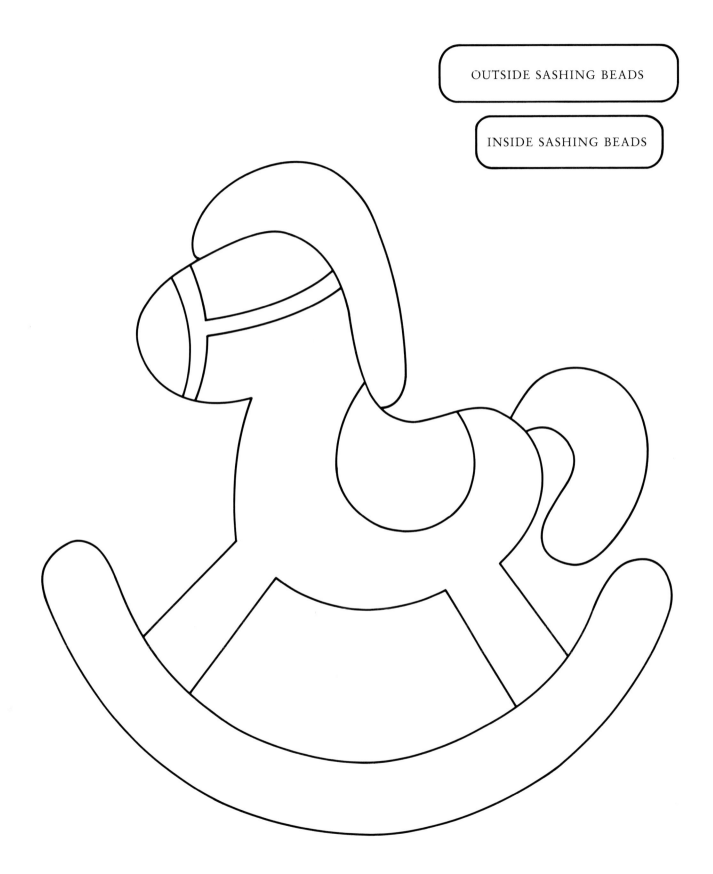

OUTSIDE SASHING BEADS

INSIDE SASHING BEADS

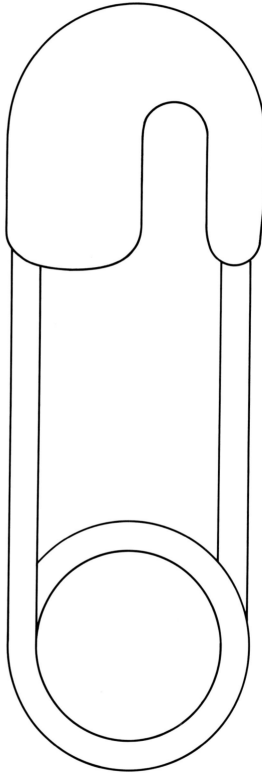

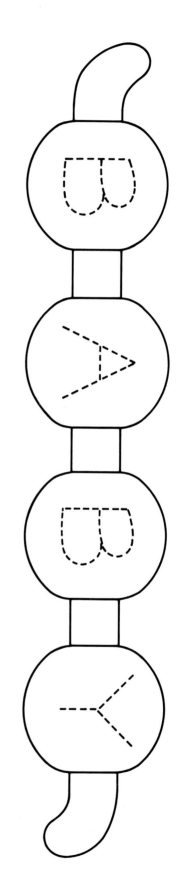

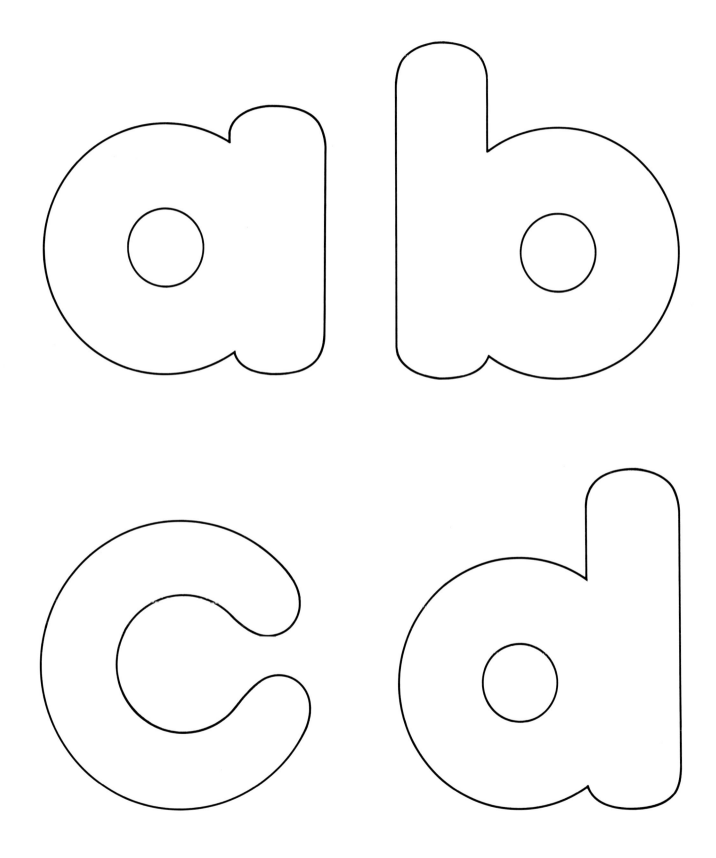

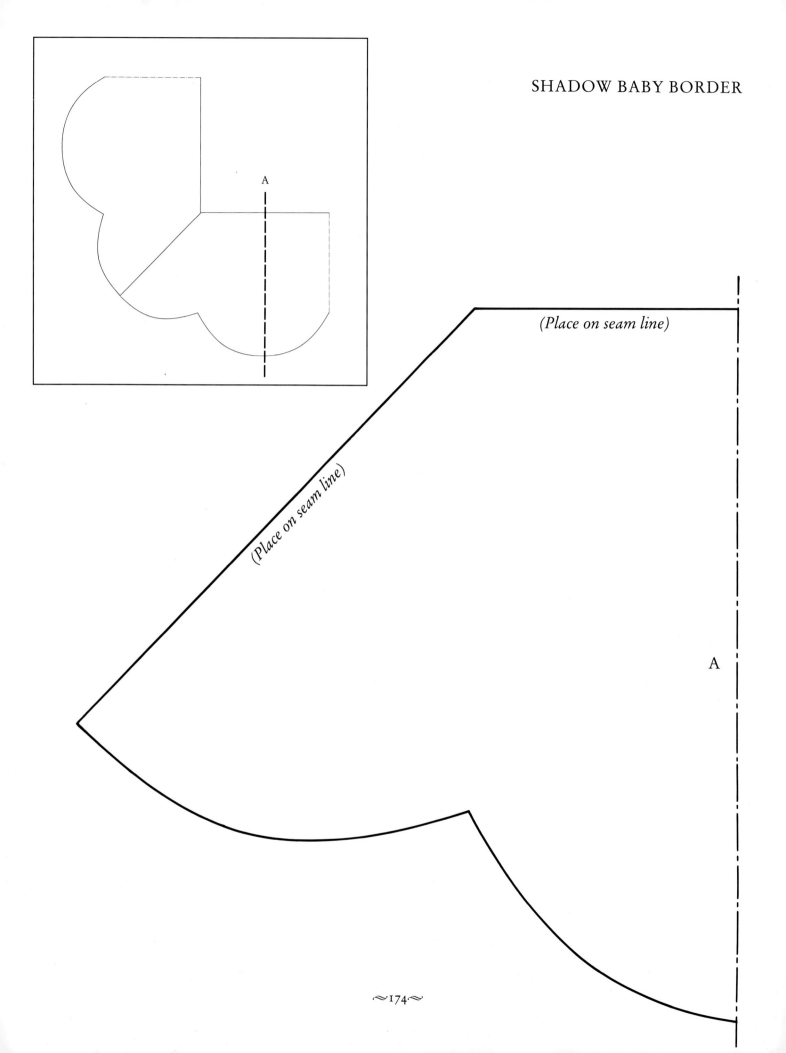

SHADOW BABY BORDER

(Place on seam line)

(Place on seam line)

A

A